NUMISMATIC NOTES AND MONOGRAPHS

Number 114

NUMISMATIC NOTES AND MONOGRAPHS
is devoted to essays and treatises on subjects relating to coins, paper money, medals and decorations.

PUBLICATION COMMITTEE

HERBERT E. IVES, *Chairman*

ALFRED R. BELLINGER

AGNES BALDWIN BRETT

THOMAS O. MABBOTT

SAWYER McA. MOSSER, *Editor*

Bank Note Reporters and Counterfeit Detectors

1826–1866

WITH A DISCOURSE ON WILDCAT BANKS AND WILDCAT BANK NOTES

By WILLIAM H. DILLISTIN

THE AMERICAN NUMISMATIC SOCIETY
BROADWAY AT 156TH STREET
NEW YORK
1949

COPYRIGHT, 1949, BY THE AMERICAN NUMISMATIC SOCIETY

THE ANTHOENSEN PRESS, PORTLAND, MAINE

Preface

FEW references are found in the many works extant on the history of money and banking to certain interesting periodicals that circulated during the most formative period in the banking history of this country. The main purpose of these publications was to report the rate of discount at which locally uncurrent bank notes would be purchased in the more important trading centers. Known as bank note reporters and counterfeit detectors, they circulated and performed an essential function during part of the State bank note era which extended from the opening of the first bank in this country in 1782 to 1866.

The National Bank Act originally passed in February, 1863, and revised in June, 1864, provided for a uniform national currency in order to displace the varied State bank notes then in circulation. Having provided for such a currency, Congress proceeded to make the issuance of State bank currency unprofitable by levying a tax of ten per centum on the amount of any such notes paid out by any bank. This prohibitive tax, effective August 1, 1866, forced the State banks to arrange for the prompt redemption of their outstanding notes and, in most cases, such banks converted into National banks. After that date the primary need for bank note reporters ceased. While a few continued in one form or another after that time and other counterfeit detectors came into existence, this history is confined mainly to the period prior to 1866.

The aim of this work is to furnish as complete a record of the subject as available source material makes possible and to shed some light on the circulating media of an important period in the nation's financial development. No such attempt appears to have been made heretofore. Many details and much descriptive matter have been included with the hope that it may contain some additional grist for the mill of the true student of banking history. It contains several references to, and descriptions of, closely related and contemporary *publications. The source material was in many cases the publications themselves, not a few of which have been personally examined by the writer.*

The compilation of this information has been an interesting task which necessitated exhaustive research in a great many places. While the utmost care has been taken to make this work as complete as possible, it is not unlikely, when taking into consideration the ephemeral nature of these publications, that omissions will be found.

Many individuals have aided the author in the preparation of this study and merit his heartfelt thanks. His appreciation is especially extended to the many libraries and historical societies which have so graciously answered his many inquiries. He will feel amply rewarded for his efforts if this work contributes in some measure to the history of banking in the United States.

WILLIAM H. DILLISTIN

Paterson, New Jersey
July 1, 1949

Contents

CHAPTER	PAGE
I. Early Banks and Bank Note Lists	1
II. Counterfeiters and Counterfeiting	10
III. Bank Note Reporters and Counterfeit Detectors	41
IV. Wildcat Banks and Wildcat Bank Notes	59
V. The Reporters and Their Publishers	78
VI. Contemporary Related Publications	141
Appendix	154
Bibliography	161
Index	165

Illustrations

PLATE			PAGES IN TEXT
I	Counterfeit Note	$5.00 The Paterson Bank	17
II	Counterfeit Note	$2.00 Newark Banking and Insurance Company	17
III	Spurious Note	$50.00 The Bank of New York	17
IV	Spurious Note	$100.00 The Bank of New York	17
V	Genuine Note	$2.00 The Central Bank of Tennessee	18
VI	Altered Note	$2.00 The Central Bank of Tennessee	18
VII	Genuine Note	$5.00 The Central Bank of Tennessee	18
VIII	Altered Note	$5.00 The Central Bank of Tennessee	18
IX	Genuine Note	$1.00 The National Bank, Paterson, New Jersey	23
X	Raised Note	$1.00 The National Bank, Paterson, New Jersey	23
XI	Genuine Note	$5.00 The Gloucester Bank (Obverse)	24, 29
XII	Genuine Note	$5.00 The Gloucester Bank (Reverse)	29
XIII	Post Note	$100.00 The North River Banking Co., New-York	69
XIV	Post Note	$2.00 The City Trust & Banking Company	69
XV	Post Note	$3.00 The Globe Bank, New-York	69
XVI	Post Note	$20.00 The New-York Loan Company	69
XVII	The Autographical Counterfeit Detector, Fifth Edition—1853		151
XVIII	Lord's Detector and Bank Note Vignette Describer, Sept. 15, 1857		122
XIX	Dye's Bank Note Plate Delineator, 1855		146

Bank Note Reporters and Counterfeit Detectors

I

EARLY BANKS AND BANK NOTE LISTS

THERE were no chartered banks in this country, as the term bank is generally understood, until the Bank of North America commenced business in Philadelphia on January 7, 1782, just eighty days after the surrender of Cornwallis at Yorktown. In 1784, the Bank of New York and the Bank of Massachusetts at Boston opened their doors for business. At the time of the adoption of the Constitution in 1787, these three banks were the only ones in operation in this country. During the next decade more than sixty other banks began operations; at least one in each state along the Eastern seaboard from Maine to South Carolina. In the early days deposits were a minor item in banking operations, the banks being banks of issue, and circulating notes which most banks issued were their chief earning medium.

As banking and trade developed and the notes issued by the many banks found their way into distant communities, need arose for a means of converting such notes into specie or available bank deposits. As a result of this need there grew up in the larger trade centers, exchange and commission brokers who would purchase, in most cases at a discount, notes issued by banks in other cities and towns. The development of this traffic in bank notes led to the publication in the newspapers of bank note lists which indicated the rate of discount at which notes of the outlying banks would be purchased by the brokers in important trading centers.

The notes issued by the early banks did not always possess the desired attribute of universal acceptability. If a Philadelphia merchant, for example, came to New York City with notes of the Bank of North America and tendered them in payment for goods purchased, the dealer in New York might not be willing to accept such notes at their face amount. As a result, merchandise brokers in the important trading centers broadened their activities to include the purchase of uncurrent bank notes, that is, notes that did not circulate freely at their face amount.

Probably the first broker to engage in this business in New York City was Jacob Reed, jun., who had a place of business at No. 10 Burling Slip, foot of John Street. In 1786, when there were but three banks in operation in this entire country, he called attention in a newspaper advertisement to the location of his store, "where every transaction in the Commission and Brokerage business is done with punctuality and precision." He went on further to state, "Cash given for Philadelphia bank notes at a moderate discount." [1]

In 1790, Francis White of Philadelphia advertised as a dealer in paper money. He also called attention to the location of his office where, "Will be negociated all kinds of Paper Money and Public Securities, . . . , and such paper money and certificates furnished as will make payment at the Land Office equal to Gold and Silver." [2]

In 1791, Manuel Noah, another broker in Philadelphia, advertised that he "Buys and Sells Continental & State Certificates, Pennsylvania and Jersey Paper Money, and all kinds of Securities of the United States, or of any particular State." [3] The "Jersey Paper Money" no doubt referred to colonial notes of New Jersey, as the first bank of New Jersey was not established until 1804.

This type of advertisement continued for many years and several of these brokers broadened their activities to engage in the sale of lottery tickets. Many such places of business later became known as lottery and exchange offices. The operators apparently occupied much the same position in the community that the leading brokers do today, and several of them later combined the sale of lottery

[1] *New-York Packet*, August 7, 1786.
[2] *Gazette of the United States* (Philadelphia), November 6, 1790.
[3] *Ibid.*, February 9, 1791.

tickets with the publication of bank note reporters and counterfeit detectors.

In 1808, Solomon Allen, the son of a missionary preacher on the frontier in New York State and engaged as a printer in Albany, began the sale of lottery tickets to add to his income. In 1815, he and his brother Moses formed a partnership to conduct a lottery and exhange office in New York City.[4] Under the style of S. and M. Allen they conducted their business at 136 Broadway, and in a newspaper advertisement called attention to the "Grand National Lottery for the opening of a canal in the City of Washington." They also advertised that "eastern and southern bills" would be received in payment of lottery tickets at par.[5] In other words, their commission on the sale of such lottery tickets would be partly absorbed by the discount they might have had to take on the conversion or sale of notes which they received. In 1815, B. Jansen, who conducted a lottery and exchange office at 11 Chatham Street, New York City, as an inducement to further the sale of lottery tickets, advertised that bank notes not current in New York City would be exchanged at a moderate premium for lottery tickets.[6] In other words, Jansen was willing to allow a premium on uncurrent notes, thereby partly absorbing his commission on the sale of lottery tickets.

The various forms of paper currency in circulation in the early days of this country were a source of great bewilderment and confusion, not only to foreigners traveling here but to our own citizens as well. Some accounts of contemporary experiences vividly illustrate the confusion that existed.

The experience of a French visitor with Georgia bank notes in 1815 was summarized as follows:

It seems the little man had arrived from Cuba, with about eight thousand dollars in gold, which by way of *security* he lodged in one of the banks of Savannah.—When he came to demand his money, he was

[4] Henrietta M. Larson, *Jay Cooke, Private Banker*, 1936, p. 27.
[5] *New York Evening Post*, April 28, 1815.
[6] *Ibid.*, August 15, 1815.

told that they did not pay specie, and he must therefore take bank notes or nothing. Being an entire stranger, and ignorant of the depreciation of paper money, arising from the refusal to pay specie, and from the erection of such an infinite number of petty banks in every obscure village without capital or character, he took the worthless rags and began his Journey northward. Every step he proceeded his money grew worse and worse, and he was now travelling on to Boston with the full conviction that by the time he got there he should be a beggar.[7]

The storekeeper as well as the broker was ever ready to exact a discount on his own part as evidenced by the following early newspaper account of an attempt to impose upon a laborer:

The traffic of buying up Bank Bills of other states at a discount has become so general, that advantage is taken of it to impose upon the poor and ignorant, by demanding a discount upon the Bills of Banks in the Northern parts of this state, which pass as current in this City as our own Bills. An instance of this kind happened no longer ago than yesterday. A poor wood sawyer received a two dollar note of the [Mohawk] Bank of Schenectady for his labour, and offered it in payment for some necessaries he had purchased for his family at a grocery and provision store. The storekeeper told him he could not take the bill unless he would allow him a discount on it. The sawyer thought he earned his money too hard, and had too many children to feed, to dispose of any part of it in that way, and returning it to the gentleman he took it from, telling him he could not pass it without giving a large discount, which he could not afford. The Bills of Schenectady Bank are as current as our own, and can be exchanged for New-York Bank city paper at any moment; a fact which this Grocer must have known. Those who thus attempt to impose upon the industrious labourer, deserve punishment as much as the man who extorts your purse from you upon the highway.[8]

In 1817, only two years after the war of 1812 had been concluded, thirty-nine families in England deputized an English writer to visit this country to ascertain whether any and what part of the United

[7] *The History of a Little Frenchman and His Bank Notes*, Philadelphia: 1815, p. 5.
[8] *New-York Evening Post*, October 5, 1815.

States would be suitable for residence. That writer, in the course of his travels in America, visited Cincinnati about November, 1817, and made these observations with respect to the banking and currency situation in that vicinity at that time:

> The town contains two chartered banks and one unchartered, all in respectable credit; a branch of "The United States Bank" is also just established there; the paper money system has gone beyond all bounds throughout the Western country. Specie of the smallest amount is rarely to be seen, and the little which does exist is chiefly *cut* Spanish dollars, which are divided into bits of 50, 25 and 12½ cents. Notes of 3¼d., 6½d., 13d. and 2s. 2d. are very common; indeed they constitute an important part of the circulating medium. I purchased Cincinnati notes in Pittsburgh at 5 per cent. discount, and Louisville notes at 7½. This does not proceed from want of faith in those banks, nor are the latter esteemed less safe than the former: the increase in discount arises from Louisville being 150 miles further distant. The same principle applies to every other town, and operates *vice versa* upon Pittsburgh. The paper of banks which are not chartered, or which are deficient in reputation, can be bought at similar distances from the place of its first circulation, at from 10 to 40 per cent. discount: had I sufficiently understood this *trade* when I landed in America, I think I could have nearly paid my expenses by merely buying in one town the notes of that to which I was going. There is no difficulty in obtaining them, as there is always a stock on hand at the shavers (brokers) and lottery offices.[9]

This same English traveler during his trip of about 5,000 miles in this country, went to a store in Washington to purchase a pair of worsted gloves which he stated were of the commonest kind and priced at half a dollar. The complications arising out of this seemingly commonplace transaction were related by him in these words:

> I presented a Philadelphia one dollar note; it would not be taken without a discount of 2½ per cent. I then tendered a Baltimore bank [note], of the same amount. This being one hundred miles nearer was accepted.

---

[9] Henry Bradshaw Fearon, *A Narrative of a Journey Through The Eastern and Western States of America*, 3d ed., London: 1819, pp. 232-233.

The store-keeper had no change; to remedy which, he took a pair of scissors and divided the note between us: I enquired if the half would pass, and being answered in the affirmative, took it without hesitation, knowing the want of specie throughout the country, and being previously familiarized with Spanish dollars cut into every variety of size. I now find that demi-notes are a common circulating medium.[10]

The brokers' advertisements previously referred to increased in number and scope as the number of banks increased, and they soon developed into what were commonly known as bank note tables and bank note lists. Such lists were published periodically in most of the newspapers throughout the country and showed merely the names of the banks, their locations, and the discount rate at which their respective notes would be purchased in the larger business centers. Lack of any centralized control over note issues led to wide fluctuations in the quantity as well as the quality of the notes as they circulated and strayed far from the places where they were issued.

In regard to discount rates, the statement was made in 1817 that, "New-York, the great commercial emporium of the United States, may best serve us as the standard place for fixing a value on the different bank notes of our country." The writer of this continued his remarks as follows:

It is well to observe, however, that the rates of exchange at New-York, do not fix the real value of the paper (in many cases) at the places where it belongs; for many banks whose notes are rated at a discount, pay specie as freely as any others—and, on the whole, the exhibit is rather calculated to shew the course of trade, *as to the notes of the good banks*, than to give a specific idea of the worth of such; . . . .[11]

The publication of bank note tables or lists had not come into very general use prior to 1818, as evidenced by a writer's comments regarding one of these lists that appeared in a Baltimore newspaper.

---

[10] *Ibid.*, pp. 287-288.
[11] *Niles' Weekly Register* (Baltimore), October 11, 1817.

Niles characterized the business as "shaving of bank notes," went on to state that the table was headed "Course of exchange," and indicated that it "may be useful to some of our readers and deserves preservation as a curiosity." That list contained the names of a few individual banks and the names of several cities in each of about twelve states together with the discount rate at which notes of the various banks in those states would be purchased by the broker who furnished the information.[12]

A week later Niles reproduced a bank note table issued by G. and R. Waite of Baltimore which firm also had offices in New York and Philadelphia. He stated that it "may be useful to our distant reader" and concerning the necessity for publishing such a table, worked himself into quite a tantrum, proclaiming: "What a business is this *shaving of bank notes!* But the misery of it is—that the loss falls upon the *productive poor,* to pamper the pride and feed the insolence of the *dronish* rich."

One of the earliest tables and probably the first to appear regularly in a newspaper of general circulation was published every Wednesday and Saturday in *The American* in New York City. The table which was entitled "Bank Note Exchange," first appeared in that paper on July 14, 1819.[13] It was corrected every Tuesday and Friday by Martin Lee, a Stock and Exchange Broker located at 44 Wall Street.

An example of conditions prevailing throughout the country in these early days is found in the following account of the financial situation in Ohio. In 1819, Ohio was comparatively a distant point from New York and reliable quotations on the notes of banks located there were not always available. An attempt was made to classify the banks on the basis of their standing in the community in the following manner:

We have for many weeks past looked in vain in the Ohio papers for

[12] *Niles,* August 8, 1818.
[13] A table entitled "Bank Note Exchange" was published in the *New-York Shipping and Commercial List* of July 18, 1817. (*See* p. 97.)

some information respecting the value of the different sorts of bank notes which are sent into this Territory from that state. A gentleman from Ohio furnished the following information. Seven banks described as Good, five as Decent, four as Middling and four were described as Good for nothing.[14]

The public soon created a demand for frequent and periodic information with respect to the discount rates on uncurrent notes. A Baltimore publication appears to have been called upon to furnish discount rates, according to the following notice:

At the request of many friends at a distance, we have prepared a list of the prices of bank notes at Baltimore, which shall be corrected and re-published occasionally, or more briefly noticed as the case may require. The price of these *commodities* is becoming pretty regular and steady, except as to the bills of bad banks, which should be uniformly rejected, except in their several neighborhoods, wherein it is presumed that their value must be known.[15]

The varying rates of discount on bank notes opened up to the banks the opportunity to buy their own notes at a discount. In Maryland special arrangements were entered into with the note brokers, and it was not unusual for a bank to have agents traveling about for this purpose. After 1818, it became illegal in Maryland for any one to buy, sell or exchange any Maryland bank notes for a sum less than their nominal value, or to employ for the purpose any broker or agent. The law was ineffective and simply added a risk charge to the price asked for such notes.[16]

The note brokers, against whom there was an almost continuous fight, were subsequently licensed to operate in Maryland. In 1841, the fight against bill brokers and note shavers was renewed. The cost of their license was raised to $3,000 yearly and the penalty for exchanging and purchasing bills without a license was fixed at $500

[14] *The American* (New York), November 17, 1819.
[15] *Niles*, September 23, 1820.
[16] Alfred Cookman Bryan, "History of State Banking in Maryland," *Johns Hopkins University Studies in History and Politics*, Ser. XVII, Nos. 1, 2, 3 (1899), p. 68.

for each offense. The banks were released from all obligation to redeem their notes in specie for any foreign or domestic broker. The next year these conditions were mitigated to a considerable extent by a reduction of the license fee to $50. This was brought about by the inconvenience arising from the mass of depreciated and uncurrent paper money, chiefly of banks of other States, which by means of the brokers could be exchanged for reliable currency.[17]

The advertisements of the note brokers, together with newspaper announcements of discount rates on paper currency increased in number and scope as the number of banks increased. Bank note tables, beginning about 1820, became a regular feature in newspapers throughout the country, with the information furnished by the brokers and corrected frequently by them.

[17] *Ibid.*, pp. 108-109.

II

COUNTERFEITERS AND COUNTERFEITING

THERE are reports of the counterfeiting of paper currency in China as early as the eleventh century, so that it is not surprising that soon after paper money appeared in this country it was counterfeited. The Bank of England, established in 1694, was not confronted with the counterfeiting of its notes until many years after it commenced business. The following account of the discovery of the first counterfeit notes by "The Old Lady of Threadneedle Street" presents an interesting report:

The day on which a forged note was first presented at the Bank of England, forms a memorable era in its history. For sixty-four years the establishment had circulated its paper with freedom; and during this period no attempt had been made to imitate it. He who takes the initiative in a new line of wrong doing has more than the simple act to answer for, and to Richard William Vaughan, a Stafford linen-draper, belongs the melancholy celebrity of having led the van in this new phase of crime, in the year 1758. The records of his life do not show want, beggary, or starvation urging him but a simple desire to seem greater than he was. By one of the artists employed, and there were several engaged on different parts of the notes, the discovery was made. The criminal had filled up to the number of twenty, and deposited them in the hands of a young lady to whom he was attached, as a proof of his wealth. There is no calculating how much longer Bank notes might have been free from imitation, had this man not shewn with what ease they might be counterfeited. From this period forged notes became common. The faculty of imitation is so great, that when the expectation of profit is added, there is little hope of restraining the destitute or the bad man from a career which adds the charm of novelty to the chance of gain. The publicity given to the fraud, the notoriety of the proceedings, and the execution of the forger, tended to excite that morbid sympathy which, up to the present day, is evinced for any extraordinary criminal. It is, therefore, possible, that if Vaughan had not been induced by circumstances to startle London with his novel crime, the idea of forging Bank notes might have been long delayed, and that some of the strange facts to be related would never have occurred.[1]

While no attempt will be made to review the complete history of counterfeiting in this country, it may be appropriate to present some of the many newspaper and other articles which show how prevalent it was during the State bank note era, and the need for some form of *counterfeit detector.*

Counterfeiting of paper money in this country began long before the inception of State bank notes. Bradford's *New-York Gazette* for March 13, 1726, contains this announcement: "Public Notice is hereby given that at Philadelphia they have found out some twelve shilling bills that are counterfeit. They are newly printed and very artfully designed."[2] Shortly thereafter the public was cautioned to beware of "false Jersey money" that was passing in Philadelphia. A detailed description of thirty shilling and three pound bills was given and the following statement was made: "It is supposed these counterfeit bills came to New York in one of the last vessels from England. A large sum is already past there."[3] The Continental currency also came under the evil eyes of the counterfeiters and many interesting accounts of their work on such currency may be found in *Historical Sketches of American Paper Currency,* Second Series, published by Henry Phillips, Jr., in 1866.

The dissemination of news about counterfeit notes in the early days was mainly through the press, and early newspapers contain many reports of counterfeits and counterfeiting. The Bank of North America in Philadelphia, which began business on January 7, 1782, was, as previously stated, the first bank organized in this country. It no doubt began issuing circulating notes shortly thereafter, as the Pennsylvania Legislature passed an act on March 17, 1782, making

---
[1] John Francis, *History of the Bank of England,* 3d ed., London: 1848, I, pp. 170-171.
[2] Henry Phillips, Jr., *Historical Sketches of the Paper Currency of the American Colonies,* First Series, Mass.: 1865, p. 16.
[3] *Ibid.,* p. 87.

it a crime "to alter, forge, or counterfeit any Bank Bill or Bank Note or tender in payment, utter, vend, exchange or barter any such forged, counterfeit or altered Bill or Note of the bank."

The counterfeiters, then as now, lost little time in bringing into circulation imitations of new currency issued by the banks and the government. As a matter of fact, only fifty days after the reduced size currency, now in use, began general circulation on June 10, 1929, a ten dollar counterfeit note of this new series was discovered. As early as 1794 the Bank of the United States and the Bank of North America in a joint announcement cautioned the public to beware of counterfeit five dollar bills of the Bank of the United States and twenty dollar bills of the Bank of North America. The notice describes how the counterfeit notes differ from genuine notes, and indicates among other things that "The Signature of J. Nixon [President of the Bank of North America], has the appearance of being written with lamp-black and oil, ..." The notice states further, "It is supposed these forgeries were committed in some of the Southern States, as all the counterfeits that have appeared, have come from thence, and two persons have been apprehended in Virginia, on suspicion of being the authors of them."[4]

In 1795, the public was warned to beware of counterfeit bills of the Bank of New York, "one of 40 dollars, and one of 5 dollars, having been detected at the Bank, ..."[5] In Boston a news item informed the public that a most barefaced species of counterfeit ten dollar bills of the Bank of the United States had been discovered in that city. It went on to state, "the paper is coarse and heavy, without a water mark, Thomas Willing's name is wretchedly imitated, ..."[6]

Newspaper publishers in general believed that news of counterfeit notes was of considerable interest to their subscribers as evidenced by the following notice:

[4] *American Daily Advertiser* (Philadelphia), August 19, 1794.
[5] *The Daily Advertiser* (New York), January 3, 1795.
[6] *The Boston Gazette* and *Weekly Republican Journal*, August 28, 1797.

Counterfeiters and Counterfeiting 13

We stopped the press to insert a piece of information which must be esteemed eminently important to the Public. It is discovered that the Twenty Dollar *Albany Bank Bills,* have been counterfeited, and many of them are in circulation. Notice to this effect has been given to the Cashier of the Bank of New York, by the Cashier of the Bank of Albany. Not having received the specific marks that distinguish the counterfeit from the genuine, we can only mention it generally, to induce greater caution.[7]

The expansion of the note issues of the banks brought about an expansion of the crime of counterfeiting, which was a source of great annoyance and considerable monetary loss. The following account of the counterfeiting of notes of the Philadelphia Bank is no doubt indicative of similar conditions in other places at that time:

So serious had this become [the crime of counterfeiting], that in July, 1808, it was determined to change the whole form of the notes, which previously had been printed in ordinary types, and a committee was appointed to procure types with special devices for printing the notes thereafter. Bank officers, and particularly the cashier, were repeatedly sent to various places to testify against counterfeiters who had been arrested. Detectives were paid for hunting the counterfeiters, and a constable in 1809 was given $15 for making an arrest, while $100 about the same time was contributed "to assist in the arrest" of a notorious counterfeiter; and the Bank also gave liberally to the constables and to funds for this purpose.[8]

Further evidence of the prevalence of counterfeiting in the early days of this country is indicated in the following account:

For many years past the people of the Eastern States have been much vexed and injured by a gang of counterfeiters, chiefly rendezvousing in *Canada*, and detection was rendered more difficult on account of the impossibility of acquiring a critical knowledge of the numerous and dif-

---

[7] *Commercial Advertiser of New York,* January 10, 1800.

[8] *The Philadelphia National Bank, A Century's Record,* 1803-1903, Philadelphia: 1903, p. 42.

ferent notes in circulation. But, latterly counterfeits to a prodigious amount have been discovered on the banks of the middle states, some of which are admirably executed. If able to obtain a list and description of them, it shall have a place in *The Register*. It is stated that three persons were taken up at Washington city a few days since, one of whom had in his possession counterfeit notes to the amount of $62,000.[9]

A few years later these comments were made: "Sundry counterfeiters of bank notes have lately found 10 or 15 years honest employment in the penitentiaries of the several states. If their morals be not corrected, they will, at least, be kept out of harm's way." [10] A week later Niles referred to a statement by a judge to a jury that, "A fatal error seems to prevail that a person receiving a counterfeit note has a right to pass it." The judge stated further, "Let the counterfeit note be crossed, so that it may not deceive any other person." [11] The crossing of a note was done by drawing one or two heavy ink lines across the note, usually from each upper corner to the opposite lower corner. When genuine notes were crossed in this manner, it indicated that such notes had been redeemed by the issuing bank. About two years later Niles stated that:

We can hardly open a newspaper without seemingly hearing a bellowing aloud of *"counterfeiters"*—*"more counterfeiters"*—*"more forgery,"* and the like. What a pity it is that society should be so much demoralized, and so villainously cheated, for the benefit of a few dronish paper-lords—less substantial than "men in buckram?" [12]

There was no absence of news items pertaining to counterfeiting as evidenced by the notice: "It is with awful feelings, indeed, that we publish the terrible list . . . , of counterfeited and spurious bank notes, collected within the last eight or nine weeks, as we happened to meet with notices of such things in the newspapers." [13]

[9] *Niles*, January 18, 1812.
[10] *Niles*, July 6, 1816.
[11] *Niles*, July 13, 1816.
[12] *Niles*, September 19, 1818.
[13] *Niles*, April 24, 1819.

Again on this same subject Niles states: "Counterfeiting goes on prosperously and presents itself in so many forms that it is exceedingly difficult to guard against it. We can hardly take up a newspaper without seeing some fresh evidence of the prostration of morals caused by the paper system."[14]

Further remarks by Niles on counterfeits were as follows:

From all parts we still hear of gangs of counterfeiters or individuals detected, "too tedious to mention." How much of moral turpitude has the "paper system" heaped upon us!—*fraud* is called *speculation* and *counterfeits* denominated "pictures"—*perjury* is excused and *forgery* considered as evidence of courage! It appears to us quite reasonable to believe that not many less than 10,000 persons—paper makers, engravers, signers, etc. wholesale dealers and retailers of counterfeit money, are wholly or in part engaged in swindling the honest people of the United States.[15]

The public should be exceedingly cautious in the receipt of bank notes, generally, unless well acquainted with them, just now. The counterfeiters who have been secretly busy for a long time, have sent a flood of spurious paper abroad, some of which so nearly represents the genuine bills, that it is exceedingly difficult to detect them.[16]

The following probably refers to the "pioneer" counterfeiter of State bank notes in this country: "According to the confession of Thomas Davis, who was lately executed in Alabama for counterfeiting, he had been 38 years [since 1785] engaged in that business, during which time he had made 600,000 to 1,000,000 of dollars."[17]

Accounts quite similar to the foregoing continued to appear in the newspapers and other publications during the entire State bank note era. It will be observed that all of them were published before a *counterfeit detector,* as such, appeared in periodical form.

It was not only with counterfeit notes that the handler of paper

[14] *Niles*, May 15, 1819.
[15] *Niles*, August 14, 1819.
[16] *Niles*, January 26, 1822.
[17] *Niles*, January 4, 1823.

money was concerned; he was also confronted in the ordinary course of business with other forms of bogus notes. It may be appropriate to describe briefly and illustrate several types of bogus notes that were foisted upon the public during the State bank note era. A *counterfeit* note has been described as one that resembles and has been copied from a genuine note. It is usually the same size, shape, pattern and similar in all respects to a genuine note. A *spurious* note has been characterized as a peculiar style of counterfeit and has been so termed due to the fact that it has been printed or engraved from an original plate although it bears no resemblance to a genuine note, except as to the name of the bank and the signatures of the officers. An *altered* note is usually one where the name of a reputable bank has been substituted for that of a suspended bank. Genuine notes upon which the amount has been raised to a higher denomination are generally referred to as *raised* notes. Further details as to several types of fraudulent notes are found in the following contemporary account:

There are now in circulation nearly four thousand counterfeit or fraudulent bills, descriptions of which are found in most Bank Note Lists. Of this number, a little over two hundred are engraved imitations of the genuine—and but few can be called good imitations—the residue being in point of general design entirely unlike the real issues of the banks whose names have been printed on them. These spurious—more properly altered—bills are generally the notes of broken or exploded banks, which were originally engraved and printed by bank note engravers for institutions supposed to be regularly organized and solvent; they consequently compare in point of engraving and general appearance with the issues of good banks. The circulating notes of many of these broken banks have been obtained after their failure, by dishonest persons, who have made a business of erasing the title and location of the broken bank, and inserting in its place, either by pasting or reprinting, the title and location of banks in good credit. The spurious bills thus made have been passed upon the public in large quantities, simply because the character of the engraving has a genuine appearance, and because few takers of paper money, comparatively, are familiar with the genuine issues of all banks.

During the past year, the circulation of these spurious notes has increased to an alarming extent, an average of no less than ten per week having made their appearance.[18]

COUNTERFEIT NOTES

Two examples of the counterfeiter's art, among many others, are briefly described in *Day's New-York Bank Note List, Counterfeit Detecter and Price Current* for August 16, 1830. The five dollar note of the Paterson Bank (Plate I) is described as "5's letter C dated May 1, 1815," and the two dollar note of the Newark Banking and Insurance Company (Plate II) as "2's letter C. Jan. 9, 1822, pay to S. Nicholas,[19] Condit, President, Beach, Cashier."

It will be noted that the latter mentioned note bears two ink lines crosswise on the face of the note. This was usually done to indicate that the note was counterfeit, although it sometimes indicated that the note had been redeemed by the issuing bank and cancelled in the manner stated. The crossing of a note to indicate that it was a counterfeit is in contrast to the present day practice of imprinting the word "counterfeit" on the face of such a note with a rubber stamp. In the days of the Suffolk Bank and the National Bank of Redemption in Boston, the word "Counterfeit" was branded on the face of such a note by means of a hot iron.

SPURIOUS NOTES

Two notes, which on their faces purport to have been issued by the Bank of New York, present good illustrations of spurious notes (*see* Plates III-IV). These notes circulated in the 1840's and later, and bear no resemblance to genuine notes of the same denominations issued by that bank. In a contemporary counterfeit detector under the name of this bank and opposite the caption "50s and

---

[18] *The Descriptive Register of Genuine Notes*, New York, Gwynne & Day: 1859, p. 7.
[19] Should have probably read "D. Nichols."

100s" may be found the bald statement "Refuse All." This was an intimation to the holders of any notes of these denominations that they should be presented to the bank so that their genuineness might be authenticated. Another counterfeit detector in referring to these same notes states: "There are no genuine fifties with 'FIFTY' covering the left margin from side to side, and there are no genuine hundreds with a large 'C' on each side of the vignette."

Altered Notes

There were many clever operators skilled in the art of altering notes. Excellent examples of their handiwork are found in notes that were originally issues of The Central Bank of Tennessee. There is illustrated (Plate V) a genuine two dollar note of that bank with the main vignette depicting wagons loaded with baled cotton and drawn by oxen and mules. There is also illustrated (Plate VI) a note of the same denomination and of the same bank from which the words "Tennessee," and "Nashville," have been erased and the words "New Jersey," and "Hightstown," respectively over-printed thereon, thus purporting that note to have been an issue of The Central Bank of Hightstown, New Jersey.

It was the practice of these unscrupulous operators to obtain, at little or no cost, notes of banks that had failed and alter them so that they appeared to be the issues of reputable banks. They paid little attention to the relationship of the vignettes to the location of the bank as will be noted from the following descriptions. There are two notes illustrated (Plates VII-VIII), the first of which is a genuine five dollar note of The Central Bank of Tennessee, while the second note was originally the issue of the same bank and altered to The Central Bank of Cherry Valley, New York. That locality was the scene of a terrible Indian massacre in 1778. The main vignette on the five dollar note showing a number of soldiers taking refuge behind a rampart of bales of cotton (The Battle of New Orleans) was in no way connected with the historic background of Cherry Valley.

The Central Bank of Alabama at Montgomery also issued a five dollar note with a vignette showing the Battle of New Orleans, according to an 1857 publication. That publication pointed out in the following manner that notes of The Central Bank of Tennessee had been altered to The Central Bank of Alabama; "5's, Altered from the Central Bank of Tennessee; vig battle of New Orleans; the officers' names, J. A. Fleming, cashier, and H. H. Hubbard, president, are different on the genuine."[20]

Another example in the altered category is a two dollar note that purports to be the issue of the Andover Bank, Andover, Massachusetts. Part of the center vignette of this note depicts a cotton plant, at the left end there is a medallion of "Old Hickory" (Andrew Jackson), and in the lower right corner may be found the state arms of Georgia. This note was originally the issue of The Southern Bank of (Bainbridge) Georgia. Other issues of this bank were widely altered.

The practice of altering notes became so widespread that *Peterson's Philadelphia Counterfeit Detector and Bank Note List* for March 1, 1860, devoted a full page to "Dangerous Alterations." Among the many descriptions of altered notes, the following are typical:

Waubeek Bank Plates

Among the many spurious notes in circulation, there are none that are more calculated to deceive than those printed from the plates of the Waubeek Bank, Nebraska, engraved by Rawdon, Wright, Hatch and Edson, New York, and which are in the finest style.

Bank of Morgan, Geo.

The plates purporting to have been engraved for this fraudulent [Georgia] concern have been altered to a number of banks throughout the country.

Farmers' Banks

The plates of the Farmers' Bank, Wickford, Rhode Island, have

---

[20] *Lord's Detector and Bank Note Vignette Describer* (Cincinnati, September 15, 1857.

been altered not only to nearly all Farmers' Banks, but also to many other Banks in various parts of the country.

Commercial Banks

Plates and notes of the broken Commercial Bank of Perth Amboy, New Jersey, are being altered to nearly every *Commercial Bank* in the United States.

Following each of the foregoing there is a brief description of the various denominations of these bogus notes. It will be observed that in each of these cases, reference has been made to "altered plates." In the first two instances, *altered notes* of those banks are known to exist.

ALTERED PLATES

Brief reference has heretofore been made to altered plates. Notes printed from such plates are less susceptible of detection than in a case where a genuine note has been altered. In the latter instance, when such a note is referred to in bank note reporters, after the description may be found this warning, "hold up to the light." By this means the holder may discern a certain thinness in the paper, particularly under the title of the bank, which in most instances indicates that the note has been altered.

In Petersons' reporter referred to above, under the heading "Union Banks," may be found this warning: "*Examine carefully* any $5 note having for a vig. a large V., with the heads of five Presidents grouped about it, ..." An extremely attractive $5 note of The Union Bank of Kinderhook (New York) dated October 7, 1858, is an excellent specimen of a note printed from the plate described. In this case, the alteration was probably accomplished by hammering out the name of the city or town in which The Union Bank was located and then engraving upon the original plate, "Kinderhook."

Altered notes and notes printed from altered plates were probably the worst hazards confronted by the merchant and the banker during the State bank note era. What little protection they had was through the bank note reporters, wherein they would find under various bank names warnings of this type:

> 20s, altered from the Tenth Ward Bank, New York.
> 5s, spurious—whaling scene in an arch.
> 10s, spurious—vig. Neptune and a lady in a car, &c.
> 5s, altered from Waubeek Bank plate.
> 500s, from genuine plates, with forged signatures.
> 20s, vig. ships under sail; unlike the genuine.

Raised Notes

Bank of The United States v. Bank of The State of Georgia

In 1819, the Bank of the United States operated a branch, among several other places, at Savannah, Georgia. In February of that year it received from the Planters' and Merchants' Bank of Huntsville, Alabama, in the ordinary course of business and intermixed with other notes, the following notes of the Bank of the State of Georgia; 40 at 100 dollars each and 58 at 50 dollars each. These notes on February 25, 1819, were deposited by the Bank of the United States with the Bank of the State of Georgia with whom it maintained a reciprocal account, their transactions between themselves being almost exclusively in the deposit of their respective notes. About nineteen days later the Bank of the State of Georgia advised the Bank of the United States that the fifty dollar notes had been altered from five dollar notes and the one hundred dollar notes had been altered from ten dollar notes, and asked that they be reimbursed for the excess amount credited to the Bank of the United States.

At that time a total sum of $6,900 was due to the Bank of the United States, which sum included $6,210, the excess amount credited to it by reason of the fact that 98 notes of the Bank of the State of Georgia had been raised. The Bank of the United States refused to comply with the request of the Bank of the State of Georgia and in order to substantiate the sum due to it, the Bank of the United

States found it necessary to bring an action in the Circuit Court of Georgia against the Bank of the State of Georgia. At the trial the Bank of the United States:

> ... offered evidence to prove, that the officers of the defendants, at the time of receiving the said altered notes, had in their possession a certain book, called the bank note register of the said Bank of the State of Georgia, wherein were registered, and recorded, the date, number, letter, amount, and payees' name, of all the notes ever issued by the said bank, by means of which, and by reference whereto, the forgeries or alterations aforesaid could have been promptly and satisfactorily detected; and further, that so far as related to the said notes purporting to be the notes of 100 dollars, all the genuine notes of the defendants of that amount in circulation on the said 25th of February, 1819, were marked with the letter A, whereas twenty-three of the notes of 100 dollars each, so received by the defendants as genuine notes, when in fact they were altered notes, bore the letters B., C., or D.[21]

Further evidence was presented by both sides and judgment was subsequently rendered for the defendants. The cause was brought, by writ of error, to the Supreme Court of the United States and Mr. Justice Story in 1825 delivered the opinion which reversed the lower court. The full opinion will not be reviewed; it may be of interest, however, to quote the following pertinent remarks of the Court:

It [Bank of the State of Georgia] is bound to know its own paper, and provide for its payment, and must be presumed to use all reasonable means, by private marks and otherwise, to secure itself against forgeries and impositions. In point of fact, it is well known, that every bank is in the habit of using secret marks, and peculiar characters, for this purpose, and of keeping a regular register of all the notes it issues, so as to guide its own discretion as to its discounts and circulation, and to enable it to detect frauds. Its own security, not less than that of the public, requires such precautions.[22]

[21] *10 Wheat.* 333, 337 (U. S. 1825).
[22] *Ibid.*, 343.

Counterfeiters and Counterfeiting

A rather crude example of a raised note was that of a one dollar note of The National Bank of Paterson. A genuine one dollar note (Plate IX) of that bank is shown along with another genuine one dollar note of the same bank (Plate X) that has been raised to ten dollars. The workmanship on the raised note is of poor quality. It will be observed that two rosettes in which the figure "10" is centered have been cut from another note or notes and pasted over the "1" at each end of the one dollar note. It will also be noted that a small printed strip of paper reading "Ten Dollars," has been pasted over the words "One Dollar," in the center directly below the title of the bank.

STOLEN NOTES

The affairs of the banker in the State bank note era were not only in jeopardy through the prevalence of counterfeit and raised notes; he was confronted at times with a certain amount of risk through the handling of stolen notes. An interesting case pertaining to stolen notes occurred in 1817 as a result of The Salem (Massachusetts) Bank receiving in the ordinary course of business $8,500 in notes of The Gloucester (Massachusetts) Bank and presenting them for payment to The Gloucester Bank about fifteen miles away. The Gloucester Bank paid the notes when presented and about two weeks later discovered that the name of its president had been forged to several of them. Subsequently The Gloucester Bank brought an action against The Salem Bank to recover the amount previously paid and at the trial Cashier Allen of The Gloucester Bank testified that many sheets of their notes had been filled up (numbered and dated) and signed by him and locked up in a desk in the business room of the bank. He testified further that the key to the desk was always kept by himself and that the notes in question had been stolen from the desk by means of false keys in October, 1817, as he supposed, and the name of President Somes had been forged by some person unknown. The notes were dated either July 1st, 1814, or April 25th or May 1st, 1815, and had been signed by the cashier, and not by the president, due to the fact that he seldom went to the bank because of ill health.

The court in rendering its opinion in this case stated that the plaintiffs were not entitled to recover, upon the ground that, by receiving and paying the notes, the plaintiffs adopted them as their own and were bound to examine them when offered for payment, and if they neglected to do so within a reasonable time, could not afterwards recover from the defendants a loss occasioned by their own negligence. In that case, no notice was given of the doubtful character of the notes until fifteen days after the receipt, and no actual averments of forgery until about fifty days. The notes were in a bundle when received, which had not been examined by the cashier until after a considerable time had elapsed. The court said further that:

> ... the true rule is, that the party receiving such notes must examine them as soon as he has opportunity, and return them immediately. If he does not, he is negligent, and negligence will defeat his right of action. This principle will apply in all cases where forged notes have been received, but certainly with more strength, when the party receiving them is the one purporting to be bound to pay. For he knows better than any other whether they are his notes or not; and if he pays them, or receives them in payment, and continues silent after he has had sufficient opportunity to examine them, he should be considered as having adopted them as his own.[23]

The Court's opinion was summarized in the following words: "Where a banking company paid notes, on which the name of the president had been forged, and neglected for fifteen days to return them, it was held that they had lost their remedy against the person from whom the notes had been received." [24]

It will be observed that the Perkins' note, referred to later (Plate XI), bears one of the dates that Cashier Allen testified had been

---
[23] Gloucester Bank v. Salem Bank, 17 Mass. 1 (1820).
[24] Ibid.

filled in on some of the stolen notes. It does not appear unreasonable to surmise that this very note may have been part of the evidence submitted in this interesting case.

Broken Bank Notes vs. Obsolete Notes

The term *broken bank* frequently used in bank note reporters, newspapers, and other publications was applied to banks that had suspended operations during the State bank note era, and notes of such banks were commonly referred to as *broken bank notes*. There has been an erroneous tendency down to the present time to refer to *all* State bank notes still in existence as broken bank notes. Such a classification does not properly describe *all* such notes. It is no doubt correct to apply that term to notes of the State banks that failed prior to 1867; it is not correct, however, to apply that term to the solvent banks that had notes outstanding after August 1, 1866. Most of the banks in the latter group complied with the statutory requirements of their respective states, which placed a time limit on the redemption of outstanding notes, and some of those banks will redeem their notes or notes issued by their predecessors when presented today, notwithstanding the fact that in most cases they are not now liable for the redemption of such notes. All such genuine notes might today more properly be collectively known as *obsolete* notes, a term which includes the notes of *broken* banks as well as those of reputable banks. The term "obsolete notes" might also be aptly applied to notes still extant of railroads, canal companies, the Confederate States of America, Southern states, and miscellaneous corporations.

The Only Sure Guide to Bank Bills

Prior to the publication of bank note reporters and counterfeit detectors in periodical form, the dissemination of news of counterfeit notes, as previously stated, was mainly through the newspapers. In the latter part of 1805, the year in which Lewis and Clark completed the first recorded journey ever made across the continent, the number of counterfeit notes in circulation prompted Messrs. Gilbert and Dean, publishers of *The Centinel* (a newspaper) in Boston, to issue a "sheet" containing a description of counterfeit bills. This is probably the earliest reference to a *counterfeit detector* and is probably the earliest broadside on this subject. The publishers, a few months later, announced that, "the Public were highly pleased therewith; and doubtless reaped much benefit." The success of the sheet was followed by the publication, under date of June, 1806, of a small twelve page pamphlet entitled, *The Only Sure Guide to Bank Bills; or Banks in New-England; with a statement of Bills Counterfeited*. Due to the early date of this publication, it seems appropriate to give a somewhat detailed description of its contents.

In the preface to this pamphlet, the proprietors refer to the success of their sheet and state that "as the days increase, so FORGERIES also increase; and to keep pace with them, it is found indispensibly necessary to renew the Descriptions, with such *alterations, amendments, and additions,* as the exigencies of the times demand." The following additional reasons for the publication of this unique pamphlet are given:

The necessity of having *Checks* against the inroads of cheats and villains, was never more apparent than of late:—For it very often happens, that the honest and industrious are robbed of their property and hard earnings, by the imposition of knavery—IGNORANT *of the method of detecting these Counterfeiters, and their accomplices,* the unwary and unsuspecting, are easily *taken in;* and to add to the aggravation, receive no remuneration for the losses they so sustain!

A SURE GUIDE to *detect* BANK BILL *Impositions,* is, therefore, a desideratum at the present day;—it is indispensibly necessary.—Such a GUIDE, will be found in the following pages. Messrs. GILBERT AND DEAN, at the urgent solicitation of many friends, and with an industry, perseverance, and correctness, that does them great credit, have *altered, amended* and *added,* considerable, to the late sheet; and their improvements, so made, are herewith presented to the Public. If *any one should* SUFFER FOR WANT OF INFORMATION, *rather than buy a pamphlet*, the blame must attach to himself alone; and he will not receive that commisseration which in justice he ought.

Gilbert and Dean announced in this guide that there were 74 banks in the United States, 49 of which were located in the New England States. It contains a list of the New England banks together with the names of the President and Cashier of each bank and the denominations of notes issued by those banks. The denominations of the notes in circulation at that time were in much greater variety than now. The Union Bank of Portsmouth, New Hampshire, for example, issued notes in denominations of 1, 2, 3, 4, 5, 6, 7, 8, 9, 10, 15, 20, and 100 dollars. The Norwich (Connecticut) Bank issued among others a 25 dollar bill and the Essex Bank of Salem (Massachusetts) issued notes in the denomination of 30 and 40 dollars.

The guide also contained a brief description of some of the counterfeit notes then in circulation. A counterfeit bill of the Lincoln and Kennebeck Bank of Wiscasset (Maine) was described as follows: "The ten's in the margin, near the vessel on the stocks, have a workshop without *windows* in the counterfeits; in the true ones the *windows* are plainly seen; paper whiter and more spungy than the true ones." In the case of the Salem (Massachusetts) Bank, the announcement was made that four and six dollar bills purporting to be the issue of that bank were in circulation bearing the fictitious signatures of the President and Cashier. The further statement was made that the bank had never issued a four dollar bill and that the six dollar bill did not bear any resemblance to the genuine ones.

A New York bank teller in 1853 stated that, "the arts of the counterfeiter have been turned to a comparatively new branch of the profession," known as the alteration of bank bills. That writer was probably not aware of the following statements made by Gilbert and Dean in 1806:

In the case of the Maine Bank, at Portland; "Fifty Dollar Bills, a few in circulation, altered from five dollars." The Nantucket Bank; "Some 2 dollar bills altered to Ten Dollars." The Norwich Bank; "One dollar bills altered to *ten*—and well done." Twenty dollar bills of the Smithfield Union Bank of Rhode Island were announced as being in circulation, having been, "altered from a *one*—execution well done, but may be discovered from the word *twenty* in *figures*, which are very much crowded together."

The publishers refer to the branch of the Bank of the United States located in Boston and state that the bills of that bank come from the original bank at Philadelphia. They further state that, "Five, ten, twenty and fifty dollar counterfeit bills of the United States bank are in circulation." Following their reference to notes of the Bank of the United States the following statement is made: "All bills in Massachusetts, under five dollars, are of an oval form, and mostly of the [Perkins] Stereotype plate, so that it is impossible to alter them to any other denomination, without immediate detection." Under the reference to notes of the Essex Bank of Salem, this statement is found: "This Bank has recently issued bills from Perkins' beautiful Stereotype." In a notice of two new banks being incorporated in Massachusetts the statement is made that, "Their bills are to be done on Perkins' Stereotype, by order of our Legislature."

In July, 1806, one month after the date shown on their guide, Gilbert and Dean issued a three page postscript containing a description of many new counterfeits that had since come to their attention. In this postscript they made the following statement: "As there appears to be a new gang of villains combined together, who are *better workmen* than their *predecessors*, we may expect to hear of more counterfeits until they get routed—and all those which come to our knowledge shall be described as far as in our power, and communicated without delay."

No further results of the labors of Messrs. Gilbert and Dean along these lines have been found and it was some twenty years after the publication of their interesting guide before a *counterfeit detector*, as such, came into general circulation.

Jacob Perkins

One individual quite conscious of the prevalence of counterfeiting was Jacob Perkins who took a prominent part in the art of banknote plate engraving in the early days of this country. Examples of his work have been referred to previously (Plates XI-XII). He was born July 9, 1766, at Newburyport, Massachusetts, and as a boy was employed by a goldsmith who made dies for copper coinage of that colony. He was a versatile inventor and among many of his creations was a machine for cutting and heading nails in one operation. He designed a plate for a one pound note for the Bank of England. About 1823, he perfected improvements in the steam engine and later established an engineering business, which was carried on by his sons after he died in London on July 30, 1849.[25]

Perkins was probably best known for his invention of a stereotype steel plate for engraving bank notes, described by him as having been "made up of fifty-seven case hardened, steel dies, an inch thick, and keyed together in a strong iron frame, which is screwed firm to a metal plate of an inch thickness."[26] It was in this manner that Perkins found means for the important substitution of steel for copper plates in engraving bank notes, thus greatly prolonging the life of the plate. He boasted of the inability of counterfeiters to imitate notes made from his plates. Notes printed from Perkins' stereotype steel plates, however, *were* counterfeited as have been practically every form of bank note issued since that time. The reverse of a note printed from one of Perkins' Patent Stereotype Steel Plates (Plate XII) shows the care exercised by him in attempting to thwart the nefarious activities of the counterfeiter. While many of the notes

[25] H. P. and M. W. Vowles, "A Study in American Ingenuity and Intrepid Pioneering," *Mechanical Engineering*, Vol. 53, No. 11, Nov. 1931, pp. 785-790.
[26] Jacob Perkins, *The Permanent Stereotype Steel Plate*, etc., Massachusetts: 1806, p. 5.

printed from plates engraved by Perkins contained various designs and configurations on the reverse, such was not the general practice, as all but a small percentage of the notes then in circulation were issued with the reverse blank. It was not until late in the State bank note era that the general practice was adopted of embellishing the backs of notes with various designs and ornamentations.

One of his observations on the subject of counterfeiting in his early day was as follows: "In the United States, the practice of counterfeiting *bank bills* has really become a branch of adventurous speculation. Not unfrequently, upon the erection of a new bank, we are presented with counterfeit bills, before we have had opportunity to examine the real." [27]

A few months after Perkins' death a writer made the following statement regarding the invention for which he was most famous:

> One of the most important of his inventions was in the engraving of bank-bills. Forty years ago counterfeiting was carried on with an audacity and a success which would seem incredible at the present time. The ease with which the clumsy engravings of the bank-bills of that day were imitated, was a temptation to every knave who could scratch copper; and counterfeits flooded the country to the serious detriment of trade. Perkins invented the stereotype check-plate, which no art of counterfeiting could match; and a security was thus given to bank paper which it had never before known.[28]

Perkins' Transfer Press

It is interesting to note the striking resemblance of the practice followed by Perkins in 1806 in the preparation of plates from which bank notes were printed and the practice now followed by our Bureau of Engraving and Printing. As a matter of fact the machine now in use, known as a transfer press, represents the evolution and

---

[27] *Ibid.*, p. 3.
[28] "Memoir of Jacob Perkins," (From *The Boston Courier*), *The Bankers' Magazine and Statistical Register*, Boston, December, 1849, Vol. IV, pp. 472-476.

refinement of the process developed by Perkins. Perkins described this process in the following words:

This principle of making plates combines engraving, etching, and an exact imitation of the most difficult parts of block work, which has never before been produced. To prevent its being copied with blocks, engraving intersecting with the block work imitation is added, which gives an impression not within the power of the artist to produce from blocks. To execute this block work imitation, a long and laborious process is necessary, the expense of which could not be reimbursed, unless a great number of impressions were wanted. Circular dies, through which is fixed an iron axle, are first prepared, then intersecting lines are indented, and letters are sunk on their edges; they are then hardened, which contracts the steel; the impression is then made by these dies on the steel or copper plates, under the pressure of a strong, double jointed, moveable lever, invented for the purpose, being a new application of that power, the lateral motions of which are produced by fixing a wrench on the axle of the circular dies, and turning it backwards and forwards, till the cross lines and letters are sufficiently raised.[29]

The present procedure in preparing plates from which paper currency is printed is described as follows:

The design is reproduced in soft steel by engravers. Separate portions, such as the portrait, vignette, ornaments and lettering, are commonly engraved separately by specialists. Each works with a steel tool known as a graver, aided by a powerful magnifying glass. The finished engraving, known as a die, is heated in cyanide of potassium and dipped in oil or brine to harden it. The die is then placed on the bed of a transfer press, and, under heavy pressure, a cylinder of soft steel, called a roll, is rolled over it. The engraving is thus transferred to the roll, in the softer metal of which the lines of the original stand out in relief. Next the steel of the roll is hardened and the design is transferred to soft steel plates, again by rolling under great pressure. These plates, with the design in the intaglio or cut-in impression as on the original die, are hardened and cleaned, and are ready for the printer. The original die

[29] Jacob Perkins, *op. cit.*, pp. 5-6

may be used to produce numerous rolls, and each roll is available to make additional plates as those in service become worn.[30]

ABEL BREWSTER

Abel Brewster, an engraver located in Philadelphia and a contemporary of Jacob Perkins, published a small pamphlet in 1810 entitled, *A Plan for Producing an Uniformity in the Ornamental Part of Bank or other Bills.* He indicated that it was useful, "where there is danger of forgery, and for furnishing the public with a convenient and infallible test for the same." He also recommended it "to the careful attention of all who would wish to promote the most effectual means for extinguishing the enormous evil of counterfeiting." In his pamphlet Brewster goes on to describe his plan and discusses a controversy he had with Perkins regarding Perkins' stereotype steel plate. Brewster claimed that Perkins had infringed upon his rights. Although Brewster stated in 1810 that "it is desirable that all Bank Bills in the United States should be uniform, in a considerable part" his suggestion, which might have reduced the amount of counterfeiting, was not adopted until a great many years later.

BANK NOTE COUNTERFEITS AND ALTERATIONS

In 1853, a bank teller of New York City, who chose to remain anonymous, published a treatise on the subject "Bank Note Counterfeits and Alterations: Their Remedy." His observations and suggestions for the prevention of these impositions have been considered of sufficient interest to warrant their inclusion in full. They were as follows:

The confidence of the people in the bank note currency of New York has never been so firm as at the present time. This confidence it is for the interest, not only of bank stockholders, but of the people everywhere, to retain and increase; and under its present general banking law, if its execution is given to competent, faithful and honest officers, confidence

[30] *Facts about United States Money*, [U. S.] Treasury Department, January, 1948, p. 5.

everywhere in its paper issues will speedily be attained. Presuming, then, that the present law of New York is a good one; that if the securities deposited for circulating notes are received with the close scrutiny the law contemplates, no loss can hereafter fall upon the holder of its currency; that the millionaire and the poorest laborer alike, whether storing away at night well filled vaults or a single note, may sleep confident that the morning light will bring with it no news of sudden calamity or base fraud, by which the accumulations of years, or the hard earned wages of a day, are made but worthless rags instead of the money they represent; that this law is really worthy of all the confidence it may receive, there still remains a formidable obstacle to the use of our present paper currency. The difficulty, today, is not so much in obtaining the confidence of the people in the genuine issues of legalized banking institutions, as in determining which are these *genuine* issues. When the counterfeiter becomes so skillful that, with his work, he deceives, not only those unacquainted with bank notes and the usual method of detecting his issues, but good judges; when even bank officers, themselves, receive false issues with false signatures of their own bank without detection, as in a late instance that came under our observation; when there are counterfeiters at work in every town, thriving in their lawless occupations, and when each issue of the press announces a new and still more ingenious result of their workmanship; there would certainly seem to be danger that the whole system of bank paper for currency may yet have to be abandoned. In such a state of things, not only duty, but imperative necessity demands of the banker a remedy against so rapidly a growing evil.

Of late the arts of the counterfeiter have been turned to a comparatively new branch of the profession. The counterfeiter, the educated in his calling, and prince among the rascals of his clique, still finds his trade full of danger and difficulty. The most ingenious of the race, in many cases, find their work, if not themselves, detected long before a "good circulation" is obtained. Their work, often prepared with great care and with expensive tools, is frequently detected and announced before enough is issued to well pay the printer. The part of their trade, therefore, known as the "alteration of bank bills" presents them with unequalled attractions. With no necessity for tools nor any of the implements of the old fashioned counterfeiter, requiring only a few easily obtained chemical substances, a fine quality of glue, and a pair of scissors, to complete their kit, a few hours will transform many an insignificant one to tens and twenties, apparently as good as ever issued. In these alterations the engraver, instead of being a hindrance, is frequently of decided service to the counterfeiter. In many instances, using the same die and vignette indiscriminately for the small denomination of one bank and the large denominations of others, the engraver has already destroyed much of the aid association might furnish in the detection of altered bills. The counterfeiter, taking advantage of this fact, and clipping, at pleasure, a die or word from one bill, with little ingenuity can change the denomination of another. To these alterations the notes of all banks are subject, and no art of the engraver has yet proved a barrier to such tricks. Not only is the prominent die that denotes the denomination entirely abstracted, and a new one replaced, but even the fine lettering of the border and the centre, with equal facility are exchanged. If the engraver uses large letters, these disciples of Lucifer either extract the impression entirely, or themselves use a similar letter for bills not provided with the preventive. Black ink, red ink, large letters, borders and stripes, although at first of good service, in the end seem to facilitate rather than retard them in the profession they so perseveringly continue to practice, and the work goes on, filling their pockets, and fleecing many an honest laborer or tradesman. Yet there seems to be, comparatively, little effort to prevent such transactions. A thorough organization among bankers, and a fund provided for the purpose of detecting the counterfeiter, an effort to use but one, and that the best, kind of bank note paper, to increase the variety of engravings so that the same vignette shall not appear upon the issues of different banks, or at least upon notes of different denominations; to lessen the number and make more uniform the registers' signatures at the state department; these things, and others that may hereafter be suggested, would do much to make the business of the counterfeiter more difficult, and to assist in his detection. To prevent the alteration of bank notes a simple remedy exists, yet untried, and which we have the confidence to believe might, if thoroughly tested, prove a perfect preventive. The bank teller detects the worst alterations from association, and, if the prominent engraving of a note is

Counterfeiters and Counterfeiting 35

well remembered, he will not be deceived though the pasting process be done with the greatest degree of nicety. If, for instance, the vignette of some one dollar bill is known to be a blacksmith, the first glance at the engraving will convey to the mind its value, let the *apparent* denomination be what it may. If then, the engraver, in making up the plate for a one dollar note, *uniformly composes* the vignette of *one* and only one prominent object, the two, three and five, in like manner, always of *two, three and five* prominent objects; the ten always of *more than five*, and the twenty of *more than ten*, no matter what these objects may be, the poorest judge of money cannot be deceived with regard to their value. The fifty, the hundred, and the thousand dollar note do not circulate so generally, and are always received with more caution, so that alterations of that kind are comparatively uncommon. In order to make the bank note still more secure, every engraving, whether large or small, at the end or between the signatures, should also denote the denomination, until to alter a bill will be to deface its whole appearance. In engraving the different denominations of a bank, the vignette of the one should always be the smallest in size, the two, three and five gradually increasing, the ten covering one half of the length of the bill, and the fifty and hundred its whole extent. By this arrangement the engraver may add much to the beauty of a set of engravings, and need use neither the large red letters nor the heavy border, which so mar the general appearance of the bank note. We believe that thus, by the help of association, a preventive against all bank note alterations may be obtained, and we hope yet to see the plan tested by engravers and new banking institutions.[31]

Some idea of the prevalence of counterfeiting in New England in 1853 may be gained from the following account:

The whole number of counterfeits, including altered, or notes raised from one to ten, &c., and alterations of bills of broken to bills of good banks, for New England is eight hundred and eighty-seven; on the banks of Massachusetts, two hundred and eighty; on the banks in Boston, seventy-eight; and on the banks in Providence the large number of one hundred and thirty-eight. Considering the amount and variety of paper circulated by these banks, that of Massachusetts alone being seven-

[31] *The Merchants' Magazine and Commercial Review*, New York: July, 1853, pp. 72-74.

teen millions, and the great number of persons engaged in business pursuits, who can have but a limited acquaintance with it, it is not surprising that the "enemy" should have "sown," in such a "field" of operation, so bountiful a supply of "tares." [32]

A Lecture on Counterfeiters and Their Tricks

Mr. John S. Dye, a prominent publisher of books and periodicals, some of which will be described later, gave a lecture in 1856 on counterfeiters and their tricks. The lecture was illustrated by a panoramic display of bank notes on a large scale, and some of his remarks were reported as follows:

Mr. Dye said, that his object in these lectures was to explain the mode of detecting all classes of bad bills. The idea of describing counterfeit notes originated with a counterfeiter in Philadelphia, and it has ever since been turned to the advantage of this class of rogues.

There had been a suspicion, he said, that bank-note engravers were the makers of counterfeit money. But this is not so. There never was but one engraver who turned counterfeiter. The counterfeiters are not so numerous now as formerly. On account of the great difficulty they have to contend with in the excellent workmanship of genuine bills, they have turned their attention to making spurious and altered bills. For these they can use one plate for all denominations of bills of every bank in America. This is done by erasing the title of the bank and names of the state and town, and leaving a blank in the place of the figures and letters.

The true way to detect a counterfeit is not always by the signatures, but by the workmanship, which is generally coarse and rough. When a man takes a bill in his hand he should look at every part of it, particularly at the imprint of the engravers. It is well to look at the letters, to see that they are well formed. Most counterfeits can be detected by the imprint alone.

The panorama now moved, and on canvas, ten by fourteen feet, was exhibited a fac-simile of a genuine five-dollar bill of the Ocean Bank. Mr. Dye pointed out the beauties of the workmanship of the note, and

[32] *Willis & Co's Bank Note List and Counterfeit Detector*, Boston: December, 1853.

said that by the shading of the letters, in ninety-nine cases out of a hundred, a person could tell a good bill from a bad one. A counterfeit five on the Ocean Bank was also exhibited on the panorama, as the difference could be easily seen, even by an unpracticed eye.

The lecturer then explained the manner in which counterfeiters make plates and bills. The last new mode is to transfer by means of white wax. Even by the folds of the dress of the figures on the vignette the work is seen to be imperfect. Counterfeiters are generally satisfied if they can produce the general features of a bill.

The best counterfeit bill that was ever made was a fifty on the State Bank of Missouri. But it was imperfect in the shading, and was detected. A counterfeit note is the hardest thing in the world to make, because it must be perfect.

A five-dollar bill on the Farmers' and Mechanics' Bank of Hartford, altered from Pontiac, Michigan, was next shown on the panorama. It was calculated to deceive all outside of the bank. It was the note of a broken bank, but the plate had been a good one, and was engraved by Rawdon, Wright & Hatch, of New York.

The next shown on the canvas was a five on the Weybosset Bank, of Providence, Rhode Island. It was a Michigan bill, with the title of a genuine bank inserted. By looking close at the shading around the lettering, it appeared broken. Everything is complete on the bill, except that the counterfeiter altered it.

The most dangerous of all, a spurious note, was then exhibited. It was a three on the Mercantile Bank, Salem, Mass. Where counterfeiters have got hold of the genuine dies, they might alter that bill to every bank in North America, without altering the title.

The lecturer said that, some years ago, a certain captain got a plate engraved in New York for the Planters' Bank of Alabama. He brought good recommendations, and as it was customary in those days to allow the banks to carry away the plates, the customer obtained possession of the plate. He went to Lexington, Kentucky, and there joined a gang of counterfeiters. As there was no Planters' Bank of Alabama, they went to St. Louis, had Alabama beaten out of the plate, and Tennessee inserted. It then read "Planters' Bank of Tennessee," and thousands of dollars were made and circulated by the villains.

The panorama next exhibited a fifty on the Providence Bank, Providence, Rhode Island. It is what is termed a raised bill. The bill is genuine in every particular except the denomination, which was altered from "one to fifty." The counterfeiters probably did this work with a penknife and pen. It is important, to detect this class of bills, to look close at the letter *s* in dollars, to see if it has been added.

Another bill represented on the canvas was a twenty on the Manufacturers' Bank, Ware, Mass. It was an altered bill, and the entire end, where the word "twenty" occurs, had been extracted by a chemical process, and the paper was left almost as white as it was originally. It can be easily detected by looking at the end piece. This was a one-dollar bill. The "one" has been scraped off, and "twenty" printed in its place, leaving a whitish appearance around the letters. It can be detected by roughness all over the face.

In the course of his remarks, Mr. Dye alluded to the great improvements which had been made by bank-note engravers in the perfection of their work, which now defies the skill of the most ingenious counterfeiters.[33]

A Summarization

The general situation with respect to counterfeits, number of banks, and the confused and anomalous condition of the State bank currency was aptly summarized by a writer in 1864 in lending support of the National Banking System. He said:

In a country like ours, where commerce is the chief pursuit, many social evils are directly attributable to radical faults in business, which are very easily corrected, and yet are allowed to exist for generations.

For example, counterfeiting is a crime alarmingly on the increase, and one which leads to others of even worse character, and its very existence is due to the business of the country which tolerates such a system of currency as that with which we are afflicted.

It is not too much to say openly, and from the results of observation and study, that our paper money, as it now exists, is an intolerable nuisance, unworthy the genius of a people making as high pretensions as Americans.

[33] *The Merchants' Magazine*, etc., New York: August, 1856.

In the State of New York are some three hundred banks, with a circulation, in June, 1863, of $32,000,000. Each bank issues notes of the various denominations from $1 to $500, and very frequently using several plates for engraving the same denomination.

In New England are over five hundred banks, issuing all sorts of notes, and in the Western and other loyal States are eight hundred more, making a total of sixteen hundred banks in the country, issuing notes.

Most of these notes are quoted at various rates of discount, from ⅛ per cent to 20, and even 40, per cent. Most of them are unbankable out of their own State; many irredeemable by reason of dangerous counterfeits; and these counterfeits in circulation by thousands—a premium on crime and rascality. Banks and brokers thrive, while the community is fleeced and annoyed.

There are no less than one thousand different kinds of bank-notes, which every business man in New York or New England is called upon to criticise and examine, and pay discount on, and suffer more or less from, in the ordinary course of trade.

We talk of the inconvenience of traveling on the continent of Europe, caused by the difference in the coins of each petty State, while the citizen of Pennsylvania or Illinois must visit the broker before he can visit New York or Massachusetts.[34]

UNIFORMITY

While, as previously stated, Abel Brewster in 1810 pointed out the desirability of a uniform currency, many years elapsed before such a program was adopted. The Comptroller of the Currency in his report for the year 1912 (p. 24) stated that the Secretary of the Treasury had approved a plan for systematizing the designs on our paper currency and simultaneously reducing the size of all notes. He stated, "It is the purpose to make the notes more artistic and at the same time to give them added security in the circumvention of counterfeiting. The number of designs will be reduced from 19 to 9."

The plans approved in 1912 did not materialize until 1929 when, for the first time with the issue of what is officially known as "New

[34] A. K. Shepard, "A National Currency," *The Merchants' Magazine and Commercial Review*, January, 1864, p. 15.

Series," new and uniform designs were adopted for all paper currency. The United States Government now prints but three types of paper money, namely, Federal Reserve Notes, Silver Certificates and United States Notes. In these three issues the principle of denominational design is strictly followed. The back designs are uniform for each denomination irrespective of kind, and are uniformly printed in green. The face designs are characteristic for each denomination as regards the important protective features and the portrait assigned to the faces is different on each denomination. It was in this manner that some uniformity in the paper currency in circulation in this country was attained.

III

BANK NOTE REPORTERS AND COUNTERFEIT DETECTORS

BANK note reporters and counterfeit detectors[1] had a two-fold purpose: (1) to show the rate of discount at which uncurrent notes would be purchased or exchanged for specie in the more important business centers, and (2) to furnish a brief description of counterfeit, spurious, altered, and raised notes. The bank note lists, as previously described, merely showed the discount rate on uncurrent bank notes. With the banks of the country operating under different State and Territorial governments, a chaotic variety of notes, regulations, and degrees of security were presented, and as trade and commerce expanded, the number of banks and the volume of circulating notes increased, thus expanding the scope of the bank note lists and the prevalence of counterfeiting.

While the bank note lists were published at regular intervals, notices with respect to counterfeits in the early days were confined mainly to the newspapers. As previously stated, Messrs. Gilbert and Dean of Boston, about 1805, published a sort of counterfeit detector which does not appear to have continued very long. It was not until about 1826 that a combined bank note list and record of counterfeits appeared at regular intervals. Its publisher, Mahlon Day, an enterprising printer and book publisher in New York City, appears to have been the pioneer in this field.

Most of the bank note reporters appeared in periodical form although a few were published in newspaper style. Some of them did not enjoy a good reputation and many contemporary writers and latter-day historians were rather critical of the services and information they offered. Owing to their ephemeral interest the issue of a previous week or month was generally cast aside when a subsequent issue was received. Because of this practice relatively few

[1] Spelled "detecter" in the title of a few of these periodicals.

issues of these publications survived. These statements have confirmation in the following notice that appeared at the top of the cover page of one of these reporters:

☞ BEWARE! – As every number of this publication will contain, in addition to the present list, a description of all NEW COUNTERFEITS, this copy of the "DETECTOR" will be of no value, and will only calculate to deceive any person who may refer to its pages, after the new number is published.[2]

One rather unique feature of these periodicals was the form in which one's subscription might be entered. As each issue was published in complete form, independent of any previous issue, it was not necessary for a subscriber to refer to previous issues. The activity of one's business would appear to dictate whether one should be a semi-weekly subscriber, or whether quotations on the rates of discount and descriptions of counterfeit notes at greater intervals might suffice. *Sheldon's North American Bank Note Detector and Commercial Reporter* of Chicago, for example, was available, in 1853, semi-weekly at $4.00, weekly at $2.00, semi-monthly at $1.50 and monthly at $1.00 per annum.

The following accounts of experiences with paper currency and the use of bank note reporters illustrates the confusion and disorder that existed.

Early in 1838, meetings of the businessmen and citizens were held in the different towns in Iowa to consider the state of the currency, and to fix the rate of discount at which the so-called "good bills" would be received in commercial transactions. The territory was also deluged at that time with innumerable counterfeits of various banks, including a large issue of counterfeits on the State Bank of Indiana, as well as a countless number of forged notes and notes of banks which had no legal existence.

[2] *Bicknell's Counterfeit Detector and Bank Note List*, Philadelphia: Vol. IX, No. 7 (July 1, 1841), p. 1.

A committee appointed at one of the Iowa meetings prescribed the following rates of discount:

At ten per cent., the notes of the Farmers' & Mechanics' Bank of Detroit, State Bank of Michigan, Farmers' and Mechanics' of St. Joseph; at fifteen per cent., the notes of the Bank of River Raisin, Erie & Kalamazoo, Clinton, Ypsilanti, Calhoun, St. Clair, Tecumseh, Washtenaw, Constantine, Macomb, Green Bay, Lake Erie & River Raisin R. R. Co., all other banks of Michigan and Wisconsin twenty-five per cent.; and the notes of *all other Banks* not receivable in the Galena Branch of the Illinois State Bank at ten per cent. discount.[3]

Mr. Charles Lyell, an Englishman, while traveling in this country, relates the following impressions of bank note reporters from his experiences in Philadelphia in January, 1842:

Wishing to borrow some books at a circulating library, I presented several dollar notes as a deposit. At home there might have been a ringing of coin upon the counter, to ascertain whether it was true or counterfeit; here the shop-woman referred to a small pamphlet, re-edited "semi-monthly," called a "Detector," and containing an interminable list of banks in all parts of the Union, with information as to their present condition, whether solvent or not, and whether paying in specie, and adding a description of "spurious notes." After a slight hesitation, the perplexed librarian shook her head, and declaring her belief that my notes were as good as any others, said, if I would promise to take them back again on my return and pay her in cash, I might have the volumes.[4]

In 1843, a writer who styled himself "A Struggling Dealer" in a letter entitled "Spurious Currency," commented on the lack of protection to the public in regard to monetary affairs and made these observations on bank note reporters:

[3] Fred D. Merritt, "The Early History of Banking in Iowa," *University of Iowa Bulletin*, No. 15 (June, 1900), p. 34.
[4] Charles Lyell, *Travels in North America in the Years 1841–2*, New York: 1852, Vol. I, p. 171.

You cannot be a stranger to the load of counterfeit money that is forced into circulation by a banditti of reckless miscreants who reap a rich harvest by manufacturing and negociating fraudulent bills; this trade is now carried on to such an extent as often to deprive the honest man of the means of support. Their plans are facilitated by what are called "Bank Note Lists or Counterfeit Detectors"—and in my opinion, only serve them in their operations, for if the dealers had not these false guides they would be more circumspect in their operations of the money they take. I look upon these publications as impudent deceivers, and if they could be suppressed, or discontinued by the trading community entirely, there would be much fewer attempts to entrap the unwary, who foolishly place too great reliance upon their honesty.[5]

As travelers in foreign countries are confronted at times with currency exchange losses when going from one country to another, so was the traveler in this country, prior to 1867, forced to take losses when State bank notes constituted our principal circulating medium.

An interesting illustration of this situation (in the 1830's) is found in a letter addressed to the Hon. John C. Calhoun, then United States Senator from South Carolina, who had been at odds with President Andrew Jackson over the rechartering of the Bank of the United States. The writer of this letter, one of a series regarding the establishment of a national bank, discussed the variations in rates of exchange between distant points in the Union, and cited several arguments in favor of a universal currency; it read as follows:

Again: as worth a thousand speculative arguments, let me give you (what is no fiction) a condensed journal of a traveller who recently left Virginia for the west. Here it is:

Started from Virginia with Virginia money—reached the Ohio River —exchanged $20 Virginia note for shin-plasters and a $3 note of the Bank of West Union—paid away the $3 note for breakfast—reached Tennessee—received a $100 Tennessee note—went back to Kentucky—

[5] *New York Herald,* January 7, 1843.

forced there to exchange the Tennessee note for $88 of Kentucky money —started home with Kentucky money. In Virginia and Maryland compelled, in order to get along, to deposit five times the amount due, and several times detained to be shaved at an enormous per cent. At Maysville, wanted Virginia money—couldn't get it. At Wheeling, exchanged $50 note, Kentucky money, for notes of the North Western Bank of Virginia—reached Fredericktown—there neither Virginia nor Kentucky money current—paid a $5 Wheeling note for breakfast and dinner—received in change two one dollar notes of some Pennsylvania bank, one dollar Baltimore and Ohio Rail Road, and balance in Good Intent shin-plasters—one hundred yards from tavern door, all the notes refused except the Baltimore and Ohio Rail Road—reached Harper's Ferry—notes of North Western Bank in worse repute there than in Maryland—deposited $10 in hands of agent—in this way reached Winchester—detained there two days in getting shaved—Kentucky money at 12 per cent., and North Western Bank at 10.[6]

The problems with which the merchant was confronted are reflected in the recollections of William Earl Dodge, a wholesale dry goods merchant in New York City and later a member of the firm of Phelps, Dodge & Co. He was born in 1805 and died in 1883. In *A Great Merchant's Recollections of Old New York*, 1818-1880, he writes as follows:

In nothing is the change more marked than between the currency used during my early business life and that now in circulation. General Jackson had put his foot on the United States Bank, and we had nothing but banks chartered by the different States. Some had careful restrictions, others hardly any. Banks were chartered with capitals as small as $50,000, with no limit to their issues; and their great object was to get a location so far from convenient access that their circulation would not easily find its way back. Most of the country banks of respectability had agencies where they redeemed their bills at rates varying, according to location, from one-eighth to three-quarters or one per cent; but the banks in other distant states had no regular place of redemption, and their issues were purchased by brokers at all rates, from three-quarters

[6] *Lowndes Letters to Calhoun*, New York: 1843, pp. 60-61.

age. A short time ago, "Bicknell's Reporter," published in Philadelphia, announced the revival of the River Raison Bank, of Munroe, Michigan; and that its notes were received by the Ohio Life and Trust Company at Cincinnati. This statement is now contradicted by the Ohio Life and Trust, and no doubt the River Raison Bank, is one of those impudent speculations which are got up in conjunction with such fraudulent prints as "Bicknell's Reporter." [10]

The Weekly Herald (New York) of November 27, 1841, reprinted an article from *The Tribune* (no date) respecting the operations of two questionable banks, a rival newspaper having been accused of "puffing" the circulation of these banks. This account goes on to state in part that "if the mechanics and working men of our city are willing to be shaved and swindled, they shall consent to it with their eyes open. We say to them now that we never have seen so bold, so shameless an attempt to shave them as in this Jacksonville [Florida] Bank operation." *The Tribune* went on to state that "we have twice been induced, by the solemn assurances of men we believed honest to give some countenance to this sort of illegitimate banking. In each instance the result was a miserable failure, with loss to ourselves and other holders of the notes." This account continues:

Now if the Rothschilds were to set up a bank at a distance, and undertake to puff its notes into circulation here, buying them in at a discount, we should say to every reader, "touch not a dollar of it!" The banker may be solvent and honest, but the system is fraudulent and ruinous.

If the Jacksonville Bank were a *bona fide* and sound institution, it ought not to think, it would not think, of circulating a dollar of its notes in this city. The simple fact that extraordinary means are taken to give its notes currency proves them unsafe. The whole proceeding bears meditated villainy in legible characters on its face.

The *Tribune* article also refers to notes of the Manufacturers' Bank of Ulster which were bought by all brokers in Wall Street at ½

[10] *The Weekly Herald*, November 6, 1841.

per cent discount, and questions the right to put such notes in circulation when they could not be redeemed at par except at their place of issue. *The Tribune* inquired further, "Is it not a grievous wrong, then, to put such money in circulation, and keep it under par merely to make a profit by shaving it? We appeal to every honest heart for an answer."

It was only a few weeks later that John Thompson's *Bank Note Reporter,* a full account of which will appear later, began publication. *The New York Herald* announced its beginning and referred to comments by one of its competitors who "attempts to discredit this new 'List,' and characterizes it as being published by 'bears.'" The account continues as follows:

> There is a reason for this attack. A few days ago, Captain Morgan, the President of the Jacksonville Bank, called upon Mr. Thompson, and asked him—"W-w-w-won't you put in the Jack-Jack-Jack-Jacksonville Bank into your list?" "No," replied Mr. T. "I shall quote no banks that have been broken, and get revived; I'll have nothing to do with any shin-plaster concerns. I mean to publish a correct and honest bank note list."...
>
> Mr. Applegate, the printer in Ann Street, had a similar scene with Mr. Thompson, and told him knowingly—"Mr. Thompson, it will be for your interest to treat the Jacksonville bank right." "I certainly shall treat it right," replied T., "and put it down among the broken banks revived for a reason." Mr. Applegate looked blank.
>
> These revivals of broken banks are too much like the revivals of some—sinners—it begets back-sliders of the very worst kind. Take care of them.

The real story back of this bank, which was chartered by the Legislature of Florida, is that it had suspended more than a year before the above dialogue took place, by an act of the Legislature of Florida annulling its charter in February, 1841.

The New York Herald for January 20, 1842, reprints an article from the *St. Augustine* (Florida) *News* of January 8 regarding the

Jacksonville Bank. This article states in part that "we have on a former occasion adverted to this Bank, and the efforts now being made, to revive the circulation of its bills, by creating in New York an impression that the institution is solvent," and continues as follows:

The New York . . . , contains the advertisements of several dealers, who offer to take its notes at par in trade, and a promise is holden out, that the bills will be redeemed by the Editor of that paper. We have not at hand, the statement which was made, when it closed, showing its liabilities—but we recollect distinctly the assertion then made, that it never had any thing like specie to redeem one tenth of its issues. These issues were excessive, and of course, the holders of its notes, suffered materially by its failing to pay them. This distress was particularly felt here and in our sister city Jacksonville, and the bills instead of being the issues of an Institution suspending alone from motives of self preservation, were then worthless promises to pay, of one utterly and absolutely insolvent. The bills are utterly valueless—scarce any portion of the stock was ever paid in, in specie, and the effort now being made to create a value for its issues in New York, is only preparatory, to their being again issued in Florida, and the men duped by their hollow promises to pay.

The New York Herald of the same date then comments editorially:

It will be seen from these facts and opinions, that everything we have ever published, warning the community against receiving the shinplasters of the Jacksonville Bank, are true to the letter. We have plenty of other facts to produce whenever Morgan, the President, is ready to bring on his action against us for the $10,000 damages. But these are certainly enough to make the community avoid all shin-plasters, particularly after the deplorable results we have just seen in Cincinnati and Louisville.

While "to puff" and "to blow" have certain synonymous characteristics, this similarity did not apply when the condition of certain banks was under discussion. Some operations pertaining to

Bank Note Reporters and Counterfeit Detectors 51

"puffing" have just been related, and the following serves to illustrate the opposite of those situations.

In 1858, the Litchfield (Connecticut) Bank suspended and in the course of an investigation, subsequent to the suspension, it was testified that a sort of "hush money" had been paid to some publishers of New York bank note detectors. The court of inquiry in its report to the Bank Commissioners summarized the situation in the following manner:

> Your petitioners further aver, that they are informed and verily believe, that large sums of money have been paid by said Litchfield Bank to bank note detectors in New York, in order to give currency to the notes of said Bank, and enhanced a fictitious value to its capital stock, and that of the money so paid; according to a memorandum furnished by the Cashier of said Bank to the President, and by him to your petitioners "there has been paid $833.66 as follows, to wit: to Monroe, $33.66; Dye $166.67; Taylor $133.33; same parties $500. more, which was added to the engraver's bill—which accounts for the bill as it stands." The cashier, E. L. Houghton, also stated that Rumsey (the first owner of the bank) agreed to pay these detectors $1,000, not to blow the bank.[11]

Major Hoyt Sherman, who was born in Ohio in 1827, settled in Des Moines, Iowa, in 1848, and was there engaged in the banking business for many years. In the 1850's, he stated: "It was a queer mess of stuff that floated around as money in that early day, and the banker who handled it had to keep himself posted, not only as to its quotable mark in the *Bank-Note Reporter*, but it was also necessary to know what particular state bonds were deposited for its redemption, their market value, which was an uncertain and fluctuating figure."[12]

Sherman described a bank note reporter in the following manner:

[11] *Litchfield Enquirer*, November 25, 1858.
[12] Hoyt Sherman, "Early Banking in Iowa," *Annals of Iowa*, 3d Series, Des Moines: Vol. V. No. 1 (April, 1901), p. 7.

The literature of the profession, at least as far as the West was concerned, was confined to the monthly publication of bank note reporters and counterfeit detectors, the principal one of which, and in fact the standard authority, was Thompson's Bank-Note Reporter, published in Wall street, New York City. Each monthly issue was closely scanned for items of interest connected with the business, new banks and their officers, others in liquidation, with the varying discounts on their notes, and especial attention was given to the description of new counterfeits, of which each issue had a number. The body of the work contained titles of banks of issue of each state, arranged alphabetically, and following the title of bank and name of president and cashier, came a list of counterfeits against the different denominations of bills of that bank, and in some cases this list was a very long one, describing dangerous issues of every size from Ones up to Fifties, and in many cases the bogus imitation resembled so closely the genuine, that the bank was compelled to call in all notes of that denomination and issue others on a new plate. The Reporter was always a familiar feature of the banking office, and placed within easy reach of the teller for frequent reference.[13]

In a paper read before the Milwaukee Bankers Club entitled "Reminiscences of Banking in Wisconsin in Early Days," H. H. Camp, president of the Milwaukee Trust Company, made these remarks regarding bank note reporters:

The merchant in his store or the peddler on the prairies would as soon think of doing their business without scales, measure, or yardstick as without a "Thompson's," or some other bank note reporter of recent date and a coin chart of all the known coins in the world. The successful dealings in the various kinds of bank note currency required great experience, for without the requisite knowledge the dealer was subject to the continual tolling of his money in every subsequent transaction. The liability for losses on money by rates of discount, however, was small, compared with the losses by counterfeit money and constantly failing banks.[14]

[13] *Ibid.*, pp. 9-10.
[14] *The American Banker*, December 2, 1896, p. 2480.

Bank Note Reporters and Counterfeit Detectors 53

In 1855, a writer appealed to the Massachusetts Legislature against the use of small bills and made these observations with respect to bank note reporters:

> ... how large a part of the community can begin to distinguish between good money and bad? Who stops even to examine? Who does not "go it blind?" Possibly if you offer a new or strange-looking bill for groceries, the grocer's boy wastes his time and yours by consulting that most popular of the monthly journals, the *Counterfeit Detector*. How that periodical grows and flourishes! It bids fair to rival Webster's Dictionary in size, and eclipse it in practical utility. Did you ever consider what this curious detective literature proves? If you see the scalps and tails of a thousand foxes nailed to a board fence, you judge that the henroosts of that neighborhood must have suffered serious depredations. If you notice that fresh ones are continually added, you may suppose that those depredations are going on still. But my comparison does not run on all fours. To make it do so, I must not suppose that scalps are nailed to the fence, or anything which proves that the thievish animals have been killed, but only that hair enough, pulled from the tail, is exhibited there to prove their existence and something of their complexion.
>
> The *Counterfeit Detector* is like a powerful optical instrument. It reveals to you, through the darkness of human hypocrisy, a dim outline landscape of a great system of counterfeiting, by which, however, you may know with perfect safety that it is nearly as extensive as our vastly ramified system of banks, and may be regarded as an image of that system reflected from the mirror of the depraved classes.[15]

A few months after *Peterson's Philadelphia Counterfeit Detector and Bank Note List* first appeared in 1858, one of his contemporaries who had been in this business nearly twenty years, and who appears to have enjoyed a good reputation as a publisher, expressed some concern regarding the competition in this business. The following account appears in his publication:

> There is quite a competition at the present time in the business of publishing COUNTERFEIT DETECTORS. New works of the kind are

[15] *An Appeal to the Legislature For an Ounce of Prevention* (Boston: 1855).

constantly springing up, with a great flourish of trumpets, puffing, advertising, "newspapering," etc. And, what is very amusing, the publishers of every new enterprise of the kind, endeavor to make the public believe that *their* work is in all respects vastly superior to *all other Detectors ever before published*—more reliable, more correct, has greater facilities, more sources of information, etc. etc., until, we should suppose, the public had learned by this time, just about the value of all such "windy" demonstrations.

The fact is, more depends upon the industry and purity of intention of the publisher and his assistants to make a good, reliable Detector, than all the facilities, correspondents, puffing, etc., that can be named. What is necessary to be done is to give all the new counterfeits, and properly to quote all banks. In these respects all honest Detectors are much alike. Sometimes one Detector may have an item or two that others have not; and then the others may have something that it has not. The principal difference consists, perhaps, in the objects which the different publishers have in view or the purposes to which, in part, they devote them. If their object is to sustain a certain clique, or party, or certain banks, in which the publisher is interested as owner, in part, or agent, and to debase or discredit others that may be rivals, then they cannot receive the confidence of the public, and are altogether unreliable.

Correct information is what the people want, unbiased by any interested motives, or improper influences. To give this, requires close attention to passing events in bank matters, careful and personal supervision, and a constant look out for counterfeits, frauds, rogues, etc.

Messrs. WORK, MC COUCH & CO., who attend to the corrections of this Detector, have as great facilities for information, and are as well posted up on bank notes and banking matters, as any other house in Philadelphia, and do a very large business in the exchange of bank bills from all parts of the country; and besides, they are not the men to attempt to bolster up any institution unworthy of credit: hence their quotations can be safely relied upon.

A good deal has been lately published in the newspapers about "BLACK MAIL DETECTORS." There may be such for aught we know; but we have no personal knowledge of any such. We have not taken any notice of this matter before, nor do we now for the purpose of accusing others; but we have thought it best to say to such as do not know us personally, (for where we are known it is not necessary), we have never allowed this Detector to be used for any such vile purposes; nor have we ever been approached more than once or twice in the twenty years that we have been in the business with any improper propositions. Perhaps the "bogus" bank makers have been unaware that all such approaches would be useless. Our sole aim has been to give the very best work of the kind that could be got up for the use and benefit of the whole public.[16]

Robert Adams, Jr., a member of Congress from Pennsylvania, in a speech before Congress made the following remarks regarding bank note reporters:

I hold in my hand Van Court's Bank Note Reporter, showing the rate of discount on different bank notes in the years 1856, 1857, and 1858. In conversations with my father, who was one of the old-time merchants of Philadelphia, I have heard him say that it was absolutely necessary for every merchant and storekeeper from one end of the land to the other to subscribe for these detectors in order that he might know the rate of discount on the money which he took over his counter. That was a tax on every merchant and storekeeper; but did the evil end there? Not at all. For, when his correspondent came to pay for the goods which he had bought, the merchant was obliged to receive his money at whatever disadvantage, because it was a question of accepting this debased currency or losing his customers.[17]

Regardless of the nature of one's business, the matter of settling debts in the currency of the period frequently presented difficult problems. A stock broker who operated in New York City in the 1850's gives an interesting account of his experience with a questionable bank note reporter. He relates the details of having sold some stock to an operator named Slocum, who, failing to make payment at the agreed time, announced that he was "in deep waters." A com-

[16] *Van Court's Counterfeit Detector, and Bank Note List*, July, 1858.
[17] *Congressional Record*, June 5, 1894, pp. 5790-5792.

promise was effected and the broker accepted Slocum's note for $1,000 in full settlement. The most interesting part of this transaction as related by the broker himself is presented herewith:

While sitting in my office, the morning before the panic of October 13th [1857], a tall, lathy man, with a bilious smile, walked in, and said that he had been informed that I held $1,000 of Slocum's paper. I produced the note in question, when he remarked again that Slocum was "dead broke," and would never pay a cent, but he wished to use the note as an offset, and was willing to pay something for it, perhaps as much as five per cent.

After the due amount of haggling, the bargain was struck at ten per cent., and my visitor counted down one hundred dollars in five's and ten's, looking suspiciously new, on the Bentonville Bank, Illinois. To my remonstrances against the character of the money, he produced, out of his coat pocket, a Bank Note Reporter, published the day before, in which, the notes of that bank were quoted at only one per cent. discount. As this rate took off but one dollar from the hundred which lay upon the table before me, nothing more was said, and the tall lathy man and note vanished through the door-way.

I hastened to the office of an acquaintance, who bought Western bank bills, and on whisking my hundred dollars over, and studying the vignettes, he gave a long doubtful whistle, and said the bills were not salable in New York, but that he would forward them to his correspondent at Chicago for redemption, though his own private opinion was, the bank was a "wild-cat," and the currency was "stump-tail and red-dog." The bills went to Chicago by express, and in due time, something like the following letter came back in reply:

Chicago, October 18th, 1857.

To . . . .   , No. . . . . Wall Street, New York.

My Dear Sir: . . . . Your valued favor of date 12th inst., received, and also package of ($100) one hundred dollars, bills of the Bentonville Bank, per express. In reply, I visited Bentonville day before yesterday, and found it a small hamlet, consisting of three houses and a grocery store, situated on a prairie, about ten miles from the railroad. The back part of the grocery store was occupied by the bank, but as this institution has now suspended operations, the President and Cashier have gone to Chicago. I saw no safe or other evidences of cash, and so conclude the assets are now in the breeches pocket of the President and Cashier.

The bills have only a nominal value in our market of from 2 to 5 per cent. We cannot, today, pay you over 2 per cent., should you wish to sell them.

My expenses to and from Bentonville were fifteen dollars, which I have charged to you.

Yours Respectfully,
C. D. CULLENDER.[18]

The *Cincinnati Gazette* (no date) presents an account of an Indiana bank in a rather picturesque manner. It relates that in June, 1859, the Cincinnati police succeeded in breaking up a bogus bank at Hartford, a town in the back country of Indiana, called the "Manufacturers' Bank," and arrested one Williams, the alleged proprietor. The article continues as follows:

The officers took an account of the "stock," which inventoried as follows: About $600 in 1's, 5's and 10's of the Manufacturers' Bank; one trunk, (which represented the "safe,") two shirts, one vest, and two sections of a flute! The entire catalogue, except the bills, was subsequently attached for a board bill due the village justice. Williams, before he knew who the officers were, (for they passed themselves off as "financiers,") explained that the bank was got up by parties in New York and Detroit; that he, Mr. Williams, was the "banker," and the only person to be known in the matter; that they paid $165 for the engraving of the bills, and that $70,000 had been printed at a cost of a quarter of a cent on the dollar; that he came to Hartford in February last to open his bank, but that the want of a few hundred dollars had hitherto prevented his opening. He further said that they had everything right with the publishers of a certain New-York Counterfeit Detector, as they had *paid them nineteen hundred dollars to quote the money right!* The bills were

[18] Wm. W. Fowler, *Ten Years in Wall Street*, Hartford: 1870, pp. 110-112.

intended to be circulated "away out West," so that it would be difficult for them to come back for redemption.[19]

The foregoing accounts tend to show the reputation and standing of bank note reporters over their relatively short period of existence. While many of the accounts related give them a bad reputation, there were several publishers whose reputation and standing was of the best and under no circumstances could they be prevailed upon to "puff" a bank or not to "blow" a bank.

[19] *The Bankers' Magazine and Statistical Register*, New York: August, 1859.

IV

WILDCAT BANKS AND WILDCAT BANK NOTES

WILDCAT banking was prevalent during most of the State bank note era and this narrative of bank note reporters would be quite incomplete without some reference to this unrestrained type of bank and the bank notes issued by them. "Wildcat" has been defined as—"not sound or safe; unreliable; irresponsible;—applied esp. to unsound business houses, enterprises or methods; as, a *wildcat* bank, mine, scheme; *wildcat* currency, such as issued by a *wildcat* bank . . ." and a "*wildcat* bank" as one which, before the enactment of the National Bank Act in 1863, issued notes in excess of its capacity to redeem them.[1] Wildcat banking was an eventful phase of our banking history and one that has not had much attention in histories of banking.

In the period prior to the expiration of the charter of the Second Bank of the United States in 1836, banking business in this country enjoyed a very distinct monopoly. A charter to operate a bank could not be obtained in most States without a special act of the legislature and the legislators were jealous of their prerogatives. The granting of bank charters under such special acts was subjected to many forms of favoritism and partisan spoils. The State frequently reserved to itself the right to subscribe for shares of stock, and substantial cash bonuses were frequently exacted.

In the late 1830's, the "free banking system" was developed, and, as the name implies, it permitted an individual or a group of individuals to engage in the banking business after complying with a few general conditions. In most States the requirements were quite unrestrictive in scope which resulted in a great increase in the number of banks in the country, many of which were organized by in-

[1] *Webster's New International Dictionary of the English Language*, 2d ed., 1945.

dividuals with little or no capital and with little or no thought in mind of serving the public.

As previously stated, the early banks were banks of issue, and the issuing of circulating notes was their principal source of profit. This was the case with most of the banks organized under the free banking laws. The first move of many organizers after getting their bank notes ready was to find a locality in which to circulate them remote from the point of issue, so that their return for redemption should be as tedious and difficult as possible. As a result of this, many of these banks were located in the depths of forests where there were few human habitations, but plenty of wildcats. Thus, as one writer describes them, they came to be known as "wild-cat banks." [2]

A rather picturesque description of a wildcat bank was given by a pioneer of Iowa in the following words:

I visited one of these banks once. It was in a logging camp in the thick woods near the east shore of Lake Michigan. It was about eight feet square, eight feet high, made of rough boards, flat roof, with one small sliding window, a plain board shelf, on which the notes were signed, a small door, over which, in red chalk, was the name of the bank. It was never occupied but once. When I saw it, the bank had closed.[3]

Hon. Millard Fillmore, Comptroller of the State of New York, in a circular dated May 2, 1848, stated that "a practice has grown up under the general banking law of establishing banks in obscure places, in remote parts of the State, where little or no business is done, with a view of obtaining a circulation merely, and doing no other business."

Another description of wildcat banks was found in the following account:

These banks were usually located in inaccessible places, many in the northern wilderness, where white men seldom trod, and only an Indian

[2] Horace White, *Money and Banking*, 5th ed., New York: 1914, p. 327.
[3] Howard H. Preston, *History of Banking in Iowa*, 1922, p. 59.

Wildcat Banks and Wildcat Bank Notes

guide could find. In some instances they were located within an Indian reservation, and had but a shanty for a bank. This condition could not long continue unmolested. The discount on the notes depended upon the "get-at-a-ble" location of the bank. The notes being redeemable in gold, were picked up, assorted, and the so-called "carpet-bagger" sent out by the brokers to demand the coin, provided he could find the bank. Sometimes, when coming too near, a woodsman on the watch would meet him, and by intimidation or threat the hunter for coin would retrace his steps without venturing to make his demand.[4]

Under date of November 15, 1857, Col. Thomas H. Benton addressed a letter to the editors of *The National Intelligencer* in which he commented upon "free banking." He said that the hard money democracy was accustomed to call that form of banking "free swindling." Anybody could become a banker that pleased, issue small notes and send them off to a distance to be circulated and lost and to sink upon the heads of the laboring people.

Benton said further that it was a favorite plan to issue notes at one place payable at another far off, and difficult to be got at, so as to compel the holder to submit to a shave. He attributed that method of doing business to a Scotchman of Aberdeen in 1806, and sarcastically commented that *he* was in Great Britain and not in the United States and that the British Ministry and the British Parliament immediately took cognizance of the inventor and his imitators and placed them all in the category of swindlers, and so put an end to their operations.[5]

Wolves, Panthers, and Wildcats

The origin of the term "wildcat" as applied to bank notes is attributed by another writer to a very early period and to a somewhat more logical source. He relates that on December 23, 1816, the Governor of Missouri Territory approved an Act, "To encourage the killing of wolves, panthers, and wildcats." The act provided that a

[4] John Jay Knox, *A History of Banking in the United States*, 1903, p. 747.
[5] *The Bankers' Magazine*, etc., New York: January, 1858, pp. 561-562.

premium be paid to any person who shall kill any wolf, panther, or wildcat within ten miles of any settlement in the territory. The rate of such premium in the case of wolves and panthers which shall exceed the age of six months being two dollars, if under that age the sum of one dollar and in the case of wildcats the sum of fifty cents each, regardless of age; to be paid out of the county treasury in which any such animal shall have been killed. The act provided further, "That any person killing a wolf, panther, or wildcat as aforesaid, shall exhibit the scalp with both ears, . . . to some justice of the peace within said county, . . ." the justice being directed to execute a certificate in the following form if he was satisfied that the exhibitor was entitled to a premium; "I, A. B. a justice of the peace, . . . do hereby certify, that the sum of .... is due to C. D. as a premium for his killing a wolf, panther or wildcat (as the case may be) and the treasurer of the county is hereby directed to pay the same to C. D. or bearer."

The most interesting part of this early act is the further provision that any such certificate "shall be a legal tender for any county taxes levied within said county, and shall be received by the sheriff or other person collecting any county levy within the same." These "wildcat certificates" came to be used as currency and led to the name of "wildcat" being given to other kinds of currency that were not redeemable in specie, and being specially applied to the bills of the non-specie paying banks in the adjoining territories.[6]

In an action against the state of Missouri a few years later with respect to the issuance of promissory notes, the following comments were made regarding another form of "certificate," in the same locale:

> The states may borrow money, and give notes; but that is not coining money, nor is it emitting bills of credit; and so "Wolf and crow scalp certificates" are only evidence that the counties in the states which

[6] Breckinridge Jones, "One Hundred Years of Banking in Missouri, 1820-1920," *The Missouri Historical Review*, Vol. XV (January, 1921, No. 2, p. 359).

authorize them owe so much money for meritorious and beneficial services.[7]

Carpet-Bags and Saddle-Bags

Another writer stated that the practice of establishing banks in isolated places in order to evade the redemption of notes also gave rise to another popular term, "saddle-bag" banks.[8] They were banks whose notes were carried about the country in saddle-bags or carpet-bags.

The State banks, in their efforts to attain profits, resorted to every possible scheme to put their notes into circulation as well as to prevent their speedy return for redemption. In a speech on *The Money Question*, delivered in August, 1875, at Indianapolis, the Hon. William D. Kelley described the efforts used by bankers to keep their notes in circulation, and gave a rather detailed description of a "carpet-bagger." Kelley was 61 years old at that time and a Member of Congress. He served as such from 1860 to the time of his death in 1890. He made a great many speeches and appears to have been a man well versed in banking and finance. The speech referred to above was published in full some three years later and his comments concerning carpet baggers were as follows:

Do you know where the phrase "carpet-bagger" came from: The younger men of our day think it was invented to describe a man from the North who went South and got an office. Oh, no; not at all. The older members of my audience will attest the truth of what I say when I state that the phrase "carpet-bagger" arose from the fact that nearly every specie basis bank had its carpet-bagger—a fellow it sent with notes by the carpet-bag full into some distant State to get them into circulation there. If he could buy cattle, corn, hogs, or something else in which there might be a profit, he was to enter into a treaty with the carpet-bagger or other officer of some bank out there for an exchange of notes. For instance: The Frogtown bank, for I am told there were banks lo-

[7] Craig *et al. v.* The State of Missouri, 4 Pet. 424 (U. S. 1830).
[8] William O. Scroggs, *A Century of Banking Progress*, New York: 1924, p. 51.

cated occasionally in almost impenetrable swamps, and in those days, you must remember, there were no telegraphs and but few railroads—the fellow from Frogtown would get way out into Skunktown, another almost inaccessible place, and he would effect an exchange of ten, twenty, or thirty thousand dollars of Frogtown bank notes for a like amount of Skunktown bank notes, and the Skunktown bankers would put off the Frogtown notes on their customers, and the Frogtown bankers would put off the Skunktown bank notes on theirs, and thus they would go on with this legitimate business to their common advantage. I am giving you a historic fact when I tell you that I first became acquainted with that term in designating those fellows who were traveling from one out-of-the-way place to another with a carpet-bag full of notes to exchange, so that the notes put in circulation in Skunktown couldn't find their way back to Frogtown, because the people in Skunktown didn't know where Frogtown was, and the people in Frogtown didn't know where Skunktown was, and if they did they couldn't get there; the people in one place couldn't get to the other to get the specie on which the notes were based. Then after the bank at Frogtown had paid out the Skunktown notes, the bank at Frogtown would refuse to receive the Skunktown notes, but it would send the holder, who was its debtor, around the corner to a broker, who would buy them at seven or nine per cent. discount, and then the broker and the bank would divide the proceeds of this gold basis transaction. That is a specimen of what was going on all over the country.[9]

In a speech before the North Carolina Bankers Association, entitled "The Resources of North Carolina," delivered in Raleigh in June, 1899, Col. Burgwyn, a National Bank Examiner, made these remarks regarding State bank circulation:

It generally came back to its home more quickly than the parent institution wanted it back. No piece of information could be more annoying to the ante-bellum banker than the news that a stranger was in town with a suspicious-looking carpet-bag in his hand; for it generally contained a bag full of notes of his bank for redemption; for which the

[9] William A. Berkey, *The Money Question. The Legal Tender Paper Money System of the United States*, 2d ed., Grand Rapids: Hart, 1878, pp. 151-152.

ubiquitous stranger demanded gold or silver or New York exchange at a premium. I believe the carpet-bagger was a familiar personage to the banking fraternity of North Carolina long before the days of reconstruction, ...[10]

BANK NOTE APPELLATIONS

Many descriptive and somewhat facetious names were applied to the varied issues of paper money during the State bank note era and most of them can no doubt be classed as part of the slang of their respective periods. While "rags" was a term quite generally applied to all forms of paper currency by the "hard money" advocates in the early part of the nineteenth century, the most common term applied to notes of the questionable banks was "wildcat."

Before the days of the wildcat banks certain Colonial notes bore descriptive names dependent upon the color of the printed scrip. The *Maryland Journal* of December 31, 1782, stated, "The House is against taking either *black* or *red* money in payment for taxes,...." In an advertisement in the same paper of January 14, 1783, the following statement was made, "Specie, State certificates, Continental State, *black* or *red* money, pork, corn, wheat or tobacco, will be taken in payment."[11]

Some of the many names applied to wildcat and other paper currency were shin-plasters, redbacks, bluebacks, greenbacks, red dog, red horse, blue pup, bob tail, rag tag, brindle pup, and stump tail. In most cases there is information available having some bearing on the derivation of those terms. The origin of the word "wildcat" as applied to banking is related by another writer to a bank in Michigan which had on some of its notes a vignette representing a panther, familiarly known there as a *wildcat*. This bank failed, having a large amount of its notes in circulation, which notes were afterwards referred to as *wildcat* money, and the bank issuing

[10] *The American Banker*, June 21, 1899, p. 1095.
[11] Richard H. Thornton, *An American Glossary*, Philadelphia: 1912, II, 730.

them as a *wildcat* bank.[12] As previously stated the more logical origin of the word "wildcat" is found in the account of the issuance of certificates of a legal tender nature as a bounty for the killing of wolves, panthers, and wildcats in Missouri in 1816.

"Shin-plaster" was referred to by the same writer as a cant term for a bank note or any paper money, and especially such as had depreciated in value. The term is said to have arisen during the Revolutionary War after the Continental currency had become almost worthless. An old soldier who possessed a quantity of it, which he could not get rid of, very philosophically used it to bandage a wounded leg. The term has more generally been used to designate notes and scrip in amounts of less than one dollar.[13]

There were several periods prior to the Civil War when such obligations were in quite general circulation, especially when banks were not on a specie paying basis. They took the form of tickets, due bills, and promissory notes and were in many instances the private obligations of merchants, manufacturers, and others whose business required them to "make change," when subsidiary silver coins had largely disappeared from circulation.

The demand for some form of fractional currency became acute at the start of the Civil War and in 1862 Congress authorized, first, the use of postage stamps for change; second, a modified form of postage stamp called postal currency; and finally, fractional paper currency in denominations corresponding to the subsidiary silver coins.[14] The highest amount outstanding of such fractional currency at any one time was slightly more than forty-nine million dollars and the report of the Secretary of the Treasury as of June 30, 1877, shows that more than twenty million dollars of such currency was still outstanding as of that date.

[12] John Russell Bartlett, *Dictionary of Americanisms*, 4th ed.; Boston: 1877, pp. 758-759.
[13] *Ibid.*, p. 583.
[14] *Coins and Currency of the United States*, Office of the Secretary of the Treasury, June 30, 1947, p. 16.

Redback money was a term applied to bank notes of certain New York banks organized under the Free Banking Act of 1838. These notes had on their backs a large red decorative stamp. The *Albany Argus* (no date) is quoted as having said that a panic existed in the early part of 1841 in New York with respect to the free banks. The article under a heading, "*Red Back associations*," stated: "The panic in relation to 'red back' notes which pervaded the public mind for several days, may be said to have reached a crisis yesterday. Down to Monday inclusive, 13 of these institutions had stopped payment. . . ."[15]

It may have been with reference to the account in the *Albany Argus* quoted above that Cashier F. E. Spinner of the Mohawk Valley Bank of Mohawk, New York, directed a letter to the editor of that journal under date of March 17, 1841. Spinner transmitted a copy of the bank's statement of condition as of March 8 and pointed out, ". . . that we could on that day have redeemed more than three-fifths of our whole circulation in specie and current funds. . . ." He also stated that, "our stockholders are of the wealthiest farmers in our county, the stock is paid in, and the institution is managed with a view to safety rather than large profits." He continued with these interesting comments:

Our stockholders are with one or two exceptions ardent and influential democrats (as indeed is the case with most of the neighboring free banks) and it is very unpleasant for me to be obliged to make explanation to them for the ungenerous flings that are daily thrown out by the democratic press against the "Red Dogs" as they seemingly call them—it certainly can do us no good either pecuniously or politically.

In closing his letter he said, "the notes of this bank have at all times been redeemed either at New York or Albany at a rate not exceeding one half of one per cent."[16]

[15] *Niles*, March 20, 1841.
[16] Letter Book, Mohawk Valley Bank, January, 1841–April, 1843.

With respect to some of the terms applied to early bank notes we find that in 1838 this statement was made: "Michigan money is thus classed—First quality, *Red Dog;* second quality, *Wild Cat;* third quality, *Catamount.* Of the best quality, it is said, it takes five pecks to make a bushel."[17] *The Brooklyn Eagle, and Kings County Democrat* for October 26, 1841, in addition to the usual Bank Note Table contains another table listing seventy New York banks under a heading entitled "Red Back Money." In this table, notes of the Mohawk Valley Bank are quoted at a discount of $5/8$ per cent. Under the New York General Banking Law of 1838 many new banks came into existence. The public did not consider notes of those banks with redbacks as safe as those issued by the old banks, and stigmatized the banks as *red dog* banks, and the currency as *red dog* money. In Michigan the term *blue pup* money was applied to bank notes having a blue stamp on their backs.[18] It is not unlikely that the "red horse," "redback," and "brindle pup" notes have a close relationship to the "red dog" money of New York. "Bluebacks" was a term commonly applied to notes of the Confederate States and "greenbacks" was the name by which the "demand notes," first issued in 1861, and the "legal tender notes," first issued in 1862, were known. The later type note, officially known as a "United States Note," still circulates with a greenback.

A Philadelphia bank note reporter in 1839 reprinted the following from the *New York Journal of Commerce* (no date):

There is an institution (City Trust and Banking Co.) under this title somewhere in this city, organized under the Free Bank Law, and which we believe put forth some bills with the Comptroller's endorsement according to the provisions of the law. It has also sent out a parcel of mongrel notes on the Mississippi plan, with the appearance of bank notes, but "payable in six months," provided that the bank can find it convenient when the notes are presented for payment. We saw half a dozen one dollar notes of this description which were sent back from Georgia,

[17] *Niles*, June 2, 1838.
[18] Bartlett, *op. cit.*, p. 518.

signed A. Abbot, Cash. J. B. Manson, Pres. They could not be sold here at any rate. So look out, and do not take for genuine "Red Dog," that which has no red about it.[19]

The notes referred to in the foregoing were known as "post notes," that is, payable at some future time and not on demand, the period frequently being three, six, nine, or twelve months. (*See* Plates XIII-XIV.) The issuing of such notes usually indicated that the bank was borrowing upon time and was probably extending its business beyond safe limits. Notes of this type were found to present peculiar temptations for unsound banking. About three months before the two dollar note that is illustrated became due, a bank note reporter entered the word "fraud" opposite the name of this company, in the column where the discount rate is usually found.[20] A post note of The Globe Bank of New York was likewise described in the same reporter, while the notes of The New-York Loan Company were described as "no sale." (*See* Plates XV-XVI.)

The following notice by Charles Corkery, a merchant of Dubuque, Iowa, appeared in the *Iowa News* of April 14, 1838. It indicates the nomenclature applied to notes originating in States to the south and east of Iowa and the light in which they were viewed by him:

NOTICE

Tis better from evil well forseen to run,
Than perish in the danger we may shun.

My specie traps and Benton bullets being exhausted, I became overpowered with "Wild Cat," and in my own defense have shut the doors of my menagerie.

Now that I have got the animal conquered, those of my old friends and customers who are in debt to me will please favor me with a few more specimens of the breed. In the future, however, I will prefer the

---

[19] *Philadelphia Reporter, Counterfeit Detector and Prices Current*, Vol. I, No. 11 (December 3, 1839).

[20] *Clark's New-England Bank Note List, and Counterfeit Bill Detector*, Boston, July 4, 1840.

Sucker, Puke or Hoosier Tame Cat, and occasionally one of the old domestic species of Buckeye or Corncracker. In a few days my doors will be thrown open to public patronage, but I will never again entrust my person or property to those crazy animalculae imported over the mountains or lakes.[21]

The Sucker, Puke, and Hoosier Tame Cat refer respectively to notes of banks in Illinois, Missouri, and Indiana. Sucker was a nickname applied throughout the West to a native of Illinois, Puke to a native of Missouri and Hoosier, the most common of the three, being the nickname given to natives of Indiana. The "old domestic species of Buckeye or Corncracker" refer respectively to notes of banks in Ohio and Kentucky, which names are still applied to natives of those states.[22]

BENTON'S BULLETS—BENTON'S MINT-DROPS

Hon. Thomas H. Benton, an American statesman of the Jacksonian epoch, was United States Senator from Missouri from 1820 to 1850. He was a "hard money" advocate and the foregoing reference to "Benton bullets" ties in rather closely to a reference at a later date to "Benton's Mint-drops." Benton's interest in hard money is well illustrated in the following extract from one of his biographies:

So persistently did he urge . . . measures for supplying hard money to the country that for a time, his opponents called him "Gold Humbug," but this opprobrium gave way to the nickname of "Old Bullion," while the gold coins which began in a few years "to shine through the interstices of the long silken purse and to be locked up safely in the farmer's trusty oaken chest" were dubbed "Benton's Mint-drops"; and more than one story has been told of his dogged and universal adherence to his principles on this subject and of repeated refusals by him to accept in change for gold what he called "a pestilential compound of lamp-black and rags, yclept governmental paper."[23]

[21] Fred D. Merritt, "The Early History of Banks in Iowa." *University of Iowa Bulletin*, No. 15 (June, 1900), p. 35.
[22] Bartlett, *op. cit.*, pp. 72, 147, 294, 501, and 677.
[23] William M. Meigs, *The Life of Thomas Hart Benton*, Philadelphia: 1904, pp. 262-263.

Referring to this same term another writer comments: "When the Hon. T. H. Benton, of Missouri, put his whole strength forward on the floor of Congress and through the press to introduce a gold currency, he accidentally called the latter mint-drops, with a slight attempt to pun. The word, however, became popular, and for many years gold coins were very largely known as Benton's mint-drops, ..."[24] The "bullet" and the "mint-drop" were probably synonymous as a bullet has been defined as a nugget of gold, a writer in 1889 having stated, "In the clay he was ... likely to strike 'bullets,' lumps ... or pockets of pure gold."[25]

Senator Benton made some interesting observations in a speech in the United States Senate (January 13, 1842) on the Cabinet plan for a Federal Exchequer. Some of his remarks on this plan follow herewith:

The report which accompanies this plan is profuse in its recommendations, and in protestations of its safety and excellence; all the phrases of the bank parlor are here rehearsed, and set out to the best advantage, to delight and captivate us. Safe and solid specie basis—sound and uniform currency—better than gold, convertible at the will of the holder—always good: such are the holyday phrases which accompany the plan, and recommend it to our favor. Why sir, does the writer of the report not know that this is the very jargon of banking? that it is the cant of Change Alley, Cheapside, Threadneedle, and Wall street? Does he not know that it is the slang upon which every Bank charter is obtained—that it is the old worn out, used up, dead and gone, slang upon which every red dog, wild cat, owl creek, coon box, and Cairo swindling shop which has disgraced our Country, obtained their charter? and that all these paid specie til they stopped?[26]

The reference to Change Alley was no doubt to a thoroughfare by that name in London which in the early part of the eighteenth

[24] M. Schele De Vere, *Americanisms, The English of the New World*, New York: 1872, p. 291.
[25] W. A. Craigie, *Dictionary of American Language on Historical Principles*, 1938, Vol. I, p. 349.
[26] *The Congressional Globe* (Appendix), January, 1842, p. 65.

century was the scene of wild gambling in stock of the South Sea Company.[27] The reference to Cheapside may have been to a busy port of call by that name on the Connecticut River near Greenfield, Massachusetts, for the many steamboats passing between Hartford, Connecticut, and Wells River, Vermont. Many a citizen invested his hard-earned money to build canals, boats and wharves. Cheapside had traders and merchants of all kinds. There were warehouses, packing houses, a tavern, hotel, bakery, stores and shops—all the elements of a prosperous business community. As late as 1846, Cheapside was doing nearly as much business as was done in Greenfield's Main Street. But like a "boom town" of the West, Cheapside's heyday was short lived. The little steamboats could not compete with the speedier transportation of the railroads. One boating company after another failed, and business gradually removed to Greenfield village. Today, Cheapside bears little trace of its thriving commerce of a century ago.[28] Another Cheapside derivation had its origin in English slang, as "He came at it by way of Cheapside," that is, little or nothing was given for it.[29] The origin of the references to owl creek, coon box, and Cairo are somewhat obscure although there was prior to 1845 a bank at Mt. Vernon, Ohio, known as Owl Creek Bank, whose notes were described in 1845 as having "no sale."[30]

Another Benton item having some bearing on this subject is a copper token about the same size as our U. S. large cent. On the obverse appears the date "1841" and a female head facing left, and not unlike that on the U. S. cent of the same period. On the reverse appears the date "1837," around the outside edge the words "Bentonian Currency," and in the center the words "Mint Drop."

[27] Eric Partridge, *A Dictionary of Slang and Unconventional English*, 2nd Ed., London: 1938, p. 10.
[28] Anniversary booklet (1822–1947), First National Bank & Trust Company of Greenfield (Massachusetts), 1947.
[29] Albert Barrere and Charles G. Leland, *A Dictionary of Slang, Jargon & Cant*, Edinburgh: 1889, Vol. I, p. 239.
[30] *Clark's New-England Bank Note List*, Boston, July, 1845.

Wildcat Banks and Wildcat Bank Notes

Certain other names for paper currency are found in these comments in the St. Louis *Daily Morning Herald* of February 18, 1853: "All the 'individual issues,' 'wild-cat rags,' 'red dogs,' 'plank road,' 'Illinois River,' and all other fraudulent and swindling shinplaster notes should be driven from the city."[31] The "plank road" reference may have pertained to notes of the Oswego & Indiana Plank Road Company and the Covington & Danville Plank Road Company, while the "Illinois River" reference was probably directed to the Illinois River Bank, at Peru City, Illinois. The names of these three organizations are found listed among a great many others in an 1858 bank note reporter under a heading entitled, "List of Broken, Closed, Failed, Fraudulent and Worthless Banks."[32]

A Western banker in a discussion as to the advisability of a uniform currency referred to "the shinplasters of Michigan, the wildcats of Georgia, of Canada and Pennsylvania, the red dogs of Indiana and Nebraska, the miserably engraved 'rags' of North Carolina and Kentucky, Missouri and Virginia, and the not-soon-to-be-forgotten 'stump-tail' of Illinois and Wisconsin. . . ."[33]

It will be noted that the Western banker ascribes certain types of notes to definite localities. He was no doubt quite familiar with the currency that circulated at that time. However, the wildcat banks were found in many other states in addition to Georgia and Pennsylvania. The red dog notes have previously been ascribed to New York rather than Indiana and Nebraska. While the derivation of "stump-tail" was not definitely established, it appears to have had a very close relationship to wildcat, and more specifically to the lynx, both of which are members of the family *Felidae*. Lynxes are found in the north temperate regions and the lynx while larger than the true wildcat is described as having among other characteristics a short stumpy tail. Under these circumstances it does not seem unreasonable to assume that the "stump-tail" notes and the

[31] Thornton, *op. cit.*, Vol. II, p. 946.
[32] *Peterson's Philadelphia Counterfeit Detector and Bank Note List*, October 1, 1858.
[33] *The Merchants' Magazine*, etc., New York: January, 1863, pp. 31-32.

"wildcat" notes are of kindred derivation. It does not appear illogical to include "bob tail" notes in the same category.

The *Chicago Tribune* in 1858, in referring to wildcat currency in the West, stated: "Minnesota is the paradise of the feline tribe. As in Michigan in earlier days, they flourish with a vigor of growth, and length of claw, and sharpness of voice, that are nowhere else attained." [34]

Another contemporary writer furnished this illustration of certain notes that were in circulation in the State bank note era:

> In the Western States they have had wild-cat and red-dog currency. To these are now added what they denote as "stump-tail currency." This term is used to signify the notes of those banks whose circulation has been based on bonds of the Southern States. Soon after the breaking out of the present rebellion, these bonds proved utterly worthless, and the banks which held them of a consequence caved in. Their issue became stump-tailed, that is, reduced to *nihil*. *Historical Magazine* [no date or location].[35]

A correspondent of the *New York Herald* in 1843 made this interesting observation with respect to certain paper currency circulating in Erie, Pennsylvania, at that time:

> We have a currency, but such a one as has never received the attention of any of our writers on money. It is called "crackee, jr.," in contradistinction from the relief notes of the Erie Bank, which were named "crackee," from a crackling sound produced with the paper when new. The new currency is issued in notes of six cents and upwards, and a considerable amount is in circulation, as I should judge by the way it is poked at every body who comes to market.[36]

SHERMAN'S MONEY DRAWER

The average handler of money today makes no distinction be-

[34] *Van Court's Counterfeit Detector and Bank Note List*, Philadelphia: April, 1858.
[35] *The Bankers' Magazine*, etc., New York: August, 1862, p. 164.
[36] *New York Herald*, June 25, 1843.

tween a Federal Reserve Note, a United States Note, or a Silver Certificate, and all notes of the same denomination are usually kept in the same compartment. The money handler in the State bank note era had to contend with a much different situation, which has been aptly described, by Hoyt Sherman, an Iowa banker in the 1850's, as follows:

> To illustrate how the bank note deposits were assorted and treated by the bankers at that interesting period, I copy literally the labels on the several compartments in an old currency tray, in which the notes were assorted as they came in, and from which the checks were paid. These labels were: Eastern Penn., N. Y. and New England, in one compartment; Ohio, Indiana and Missouri, in another; then Va., Md. and Ky.; in another Ill. and Wis., and lastly, Western Mixed.
>
> The first named notes were choice par funds, rating next to gold, and they were shipped to New York for exchange purposes. The next two (O., Ind., Mo., Va., Md. and Ky.) were "bankable funds," so-called, and graded as among the safest of bank notes. "Illinois and Wisconsin" took in the few legitimate free banks in those states, located principally in Chicago and Milwaukee; but the last label was more comprehensive than all the others put together. It included "rag tag and bob-tail," everything not comprehended under the other labels but resembling a bank note. "Western Mixed" was the dignified and formal name for it. Its pet names were "stump-tail," "red-horse," "wild-cat," "brindle-pup," and many others of like endearing character. The vigilant banker watched that pile of currency closer than the others. Its increase in quantity caused much anxious concern—and its decrease corresponding elation. As the close of the business day approached, if the supply was large, he prayed inwardly for checks to come in for payment; and if he could close up with that part of his tray empty, his sleep that night would be calm and peaceful. That kind of money reversed the usual order of things in the mind of a banker—a large balance, instead of being a source of satisfaction, was a very disagreeable menace.[37]

[37] Hoyt Sherman, "Early Banking in Iowa," *Annals of Iowa*, 3d Series, Des Moines: April, 1901, Vol. V, No. 1, p. 7.

Some New Jersey Wildcats

Wildcat banking was by no means confined to the West. There were several localities in New Jersey where wildcat banks were established, the principal places having been Tom's River and Cape May. In 1851, two such banks in the first named community and one in a near-by town were the subject of the following account:

There is a small locality in New Jersey, under the name of Tom's River, within about a day's journey from New York [seventy miles by road] which has been selected as the nominal place of issue of two Wall Street banks, in addition to one in the immediate neighborhood,—at the Bergen Iron Works [now Lakewood]. From this circumstance, the place derives some interest to us of New York, and it seems desirable to make known that the town or village contains four stores, one public house, and *two banks*, besides the one in the neighborhood. The landlord of the public house is the president of one of the banks,—the Union Bank, Ocean County,—and the keeper of the dry-goods store, which, like all small country stores, is an *omnium gatherum*, having for sale almost every description of articles, is the president of the other,—the Delaware and Hudson Bank, Ocean County. This out-of-the-way place presents several difficulties in the way of the redemption of the bills.

The bills are mostly issued in Wall Street, and sold largely to brokers at a discount, to put them in circulation. Leaving the city at an early hour in the morning, and taking the train by the Amboy Railroad, the locality cannot be reached before six o'clock in the evening,—after banking hours. To present them for payment, it is necessary to remain a day there, as the train passes before banking business commences, and a third day must pass before New York can be again reached.

By the banking law of New Jersey, banks are entitled to three days' grace in redeeming their notes, after presentation; which enables the officers to send to New York for specie, if any large amount of bills is presented for payment. In this manner is working the trade in a depreciated currency, which is on the increase, and which it behooves the State of New Jersey to remedy.

The bank neighboring those at Tom's River is the Ocean Bank, at

Bergen Iron Works. The bills issued are a *fac-simile* of the issues of the bank of the same name in this city, the names of the officers excepted. This bank has been generally supposed to be located at Bergen [now a part of Jersey City] in that part of New Jersey neighboring New York, but this is not so.

The trade driven in these bills is all in small notes, and the only effectual remedy seems to be not to permit issues of bills under ten dollars, which our abundant supply of gold enables us to do with ease. A large profit is derived by a few owners or banks out of the New York public, for the circulation is confined to New York. The community wants no such circulation as this, and the sooner it gets rid of it the better. The issues are based on deposits of good stocks, so that, as long as the securities are of value, the bills will be of value, minus ⅝ per cent, which is the discount they bear in the market.[38]

The Union Bank at Tom's River had an authorized capital stock of 20,000 shares of a par value of $25 each, of which 19,993 shares were subscribed for by one Benjamin Snyder of Bergen Iron Works. The Ocean Bank at Bergen Iron Works had the same authorized capital stock of which 19,993 shares were subscribed for by one John L. Snyder of Bergen Iron Works. In the case of the Delaware and Hudson Bank at Tom's River, referred to in the foregoing article, it had an authorized capital stock of $500,000 divided into 5,000 shares of a par value of $100 each, of which 3,940 shares were subscribed for by one James E. Kelley who was a broker in 1849-1850 and located at 52 Wall Street, New York City. No one of these three banks had an existence of more than three or four years.

Wildcat banking as such came to an end in 1866, when the Federal tax of ten per centum on the amount of State bank notes paid out by any bank became effective. That tax forced those previously unrestrained banks as well as reputable banks to provide for the redemption of their outstanding circulation, and as a result of that prohibitive tax most of the State banks then operating converted into national banks or went into voluntary liquidation.

[38] *The Bankers' Magazine*, etc., New York: August, 1851, pp. 159-160.

V

THE REPORTERS AND THEIR PUBLISHERS

THE publishers of these periodicals had a more or less important place in the bank history of this country for the period in which they operated, and it appears appropriate to set forth in considerable detail information concerning them and their publications.

In the following pages, beginning with New York City and following with other cities in alphabetical sequence, will be found the names of all bank note reporters that have come to the writer's attention, together with other information of more or less importance bearing on the history of these reporters and their publishers.

John Thompson

A publisher of a bank note reporter whose fame in his day was no doubt greater than that of any other publisher of these interesting periodicals was John Thompson, a farm boy and a son and grandson of Revolutionary soldiers. While not the pioneer in this field, he was without question the most prominent. He was born on the family farm near Peru, about five miles north of Pittsfield, Massachusetts, on November 27, 1802, and was raised to the old New England maxim that the only road to prosperity was through hard work, plenty of it, honest trading, and thrift. John did his share of farm work in the summer and went to school in the winter. He finished his education at the age of nineteen, moved to Albany for a short time and while still in his twenties established himself in Poughkeepsie, New York.[1] He taught at a private school for a time in Poughkeepsie and in 1828 advertised as a dealer in lottery tickets, having obtained the agency there for the Yates and McIntyre lotteries. Dealers of this sort occupied much the same position in the

[1] *American Banker*, Centennial Edition, June 15, 1936, Section Three, p. 3.

community that the leading brokers do today, and the transition from the lottery business to certain banking activities was not unnatural, for all lottery men advertised to deal in uncurrent bank notes and became expert in discounts and in detecting counterfeits.[2] While Thompson's transition to the banking business did not occur until several years later, he did have the urge to move into a larger field.

It was in the year 1832 that John Thompson decided to transfer his activities to the metropolis of America. That year was a rather significant one in American banking history. Andrew Jackson had been re-elected by a large majority to the presidency of the United States over Henry Clay, his chief opponent, their political battle having raged over the question of rechartering the second Bank of the United States. Thompson's leanings toward financial affairs naturally led him to Wall Street, repeatedly the scene of incidents of peculiar historical significance. It was the seat of fashion and fine homes in its earlier years, as well as of the State government at one time, and also for a while of Congress. In Federal Hall at the northeast corner of Wall and Broad Streets, George Washington on April 30, 1789, took the oath of office as the first president of the United States. It was directly opposite Federal Hall that Thompson established his first place of business in New York City. The address, 12 Wall Street, then on the south side of the street just east of Broad Street, was approximately at the east end of the plot now occupied by J. P. Morgan & Co., Incorporated, and now known as 23 Wall Street.[3]

A brief description of his first place of business in New York City and of downtown New York at that time is found in these, his own words:

It was in 1832 that I opened my broker's office in Wall Street. The place was small and unpretentious, and would serve only as an ante-

[2] Edmund Platt, *The Eagle's History of Poughkeepsie*, 1905, p. 107.
[3] Street numbers were changed about 1845.

room or cloakroom for some of the large and elegant offices of the latter-day financial kings of the famous thoroughfare. Adjoining it was the office of the *Courier and Inquirer*, then the leading newspaper of New York. The Battery and Bowling Green were then the fashionable neighborhoods. At that time the financial and commercial portion of the city, was entirely south of the City Hall and almost entirely east of Broadway. Broad and Nassau Streets were badly paved and were not occupied either by brokers or bankers, but Wall Street then, as now, was the money center of the city and of the country.[4]

The foregoing statement was said to have been from "his reminiscences, which are soon to be published...." Unfortunately his reminiscences do not appear to have been published.

When Thompson established his business in New York City, eighteen commercial banks were in operation, ten of which were located on Wall Street within a stone's throw of his office. The Mechanics' Bank of the City of New York was at No. 16 (now 35); The Phoenix Bank of New York operated at No. 24 (now 41); directly opposite his office at No. 13 (now 32) National Bank of the City of New York was located; about next door to that bank at No. 15½, a branch of the Bank of the United States was in operation; at No. 17 (now 34) Union Bank of the City of New York had its office; at No. 23 (now 40) was and is now the location of the Bank of the Manhattan Company; at No. 25 (now 42) The Merchants' Bank in the City of New York carried on its business; on the northwest corner of Wall and William Streets The Bank of America operated; the northeast corner of the same streets was the location of the Bank of New York (now Bank of New York and Fifth Avenue Bank); and a few doors to the east was located City Bank of New York, now The National City Bank of New York, whose head office is now directly opposite its location in 1832.

Thompson, as a dealer and broker in uncurrent bank notes, was not very popular with the banks. The main source of profit to the

[4] *The Bankers' Magazine*, etc., New York: June, 1891, p. 989.

banks was circulation, and the more notes a bank kept out and in circulation, the greater was the bank's profit. Many of them were reluctant to redeem their notes in specie (gold or silver), when it could be avoided. Thompson, in buying up uncurrent notes, naturally paid for them in specie and in order to obtain more specie, to continue in business, his representatives would present such notes to the issuing banks for redemption. He had messengers in his employ who went out into the country for that purpose. In at least one instance he resorted to litigation to force a bank to redeem its own notes in specie. The following is a report of one such experience.

John Thompson vs. The Union Bank

Thompson had a 500 dollar note of the Union Bank of the City of New York, located directly opposite his office. A boy in Thompson's employ on October 14, 1835, at about 10:30 A.M., presented this note to the teller for redemption in specie. He was told by the teller that the porter was then out, and that he could not be paid until the porter returned. In those days the porter was an important individual in the bank as most of the bank's specie was under his control. It was the porter's duty to estimate the bank's daily demands for specie and keep the teller supplied. In this instance the porter returned to the bank after the boy had waited about half an hour, and when the boy asked him for specie, he (the porter) announced that he had to go out again and would return soon. The boy then returned to Thompson's office. Shortly thereafter Thompson went over to the bank himself and made some angry observations on the note not having been paid. Thompson then placed the note in the hands of Mr. Crooke, a notary, who went to the bank about noon and demanded specie for the note. The teller took the note and placed it under a saucer, and told Mr. Crooke that the porter was weighing specie and that the note would be paid before two o'clock. Mr. Crooke then asked the teller if he declined paying the note, to which the teller replied, "I do not decline it, but decline having any further conversation with you." Mr. Crooke then took the note away and protested it for non-payment.

Thompson subsequently brought an action against the Union Bank and a representative of the bank testified at the trial that provision was made every morning for specie payments during the day, and that the usual amount of specie had been brought up that morning, but that part of it was exhausted before Thompson sent for payment of his note. There was further testimony to the effect that Thompson's boy had been paid a note for 100 dollars, prior to going with the note of 500 dollars. It also appeared that Thompson was in the habit of sending to the bank for specie, and that special care was taken by the bank to have it ready to meet his demands. This was not the situation in this instance. Evidence was adduced to show that Thompson was hostile to the bank, and had endeavored to harass and annoy it, and it appeared that there had been an unfriendly feeling between the parties before the transaction occurred which caused this suit.

The court subsequently charged the jury that this was an action against the Union Bank for non-payment of one of their notes. The notes were in the common form, by which the bank promised to pay the sum mentioned in it on demand, and the first question was, What is the obligation which such a note imposes on the bank? and the second question was, Had the bank refused to pay the note in such a way to render them responsible? That Mr. Thompson being the *bearer* of the note was entitled to be paid, there could be no doubt, as such were the precise words of the contract. The question was then, whether the words in the note bore any precise import differing from the common acceptation in which the words were understood; or whether the words "on demand" mean a different period of time, when used in relation to one individual holding the notes of another. The jury rendered a verdict in Thompson's favor for 500 dollars, with interest and costs.[5]

[5] *Niles*, April 16, 1836.

Thompson as a Publisher

Little is known of Thompson's first ten years in New York City. He did however establish himself as an exchange broker and built up a good reputation as a dealer in uncurrent bank notes. During this decade he was located at no less than three different places on Wall Street and when he branched out as a publisher his address was 52 Wall Street, which at that time was on the north side of the street about midway between William and Pearl Streets.

Early in 1842 when there were only two other bank note reporters of any importance published in New York City, John Thompson entered that field. One of the then publishers was Archibald McIntyre who had previously been a member of the firm that Thompson represented some fifteen years prior thereto as their agent in the sale of lottery tickets in Poughkeepsie. The first announcement of the publication of Thompson's reporter appeared in the *New-York American* for December 31, 1841. It read as follows:

Prospectus
of a New Bank Note Reporter,
To be issued on Tuesday, Jan. 4, 1842.

From the frequent complaints of want of confidence in the existing publications, the subscriber is induced to offer to the public a new Weekly Paper, under the title of THOMPSON'S BANK NOTE REPORTER, in pamphlet form, containing sixteen pages.

This paper will give a more perfect report of Banks, Bank Notes, Broken Banks, Counterfeit Notes, and Uncurrent Money, than any other paper now published. It will also contain full and accurate tables of gold and silver coin, stocks, &c. &c.

The rates of Uncurrent Money, and Bills of Broken Banks, will be quoted with the greatest accuracy, the market value in Wall street, at the time, being always the standard.

Fraudulent and unsafe Banks will be pointed out, and the public put on their guard, where failures may be expected, regardless alike of the favor or ill-will of the great financiers.

84   Bank Note Reporters and Counterfeit Detectors

The Reporter will be issued regularly on Saturday morning, but when anything transpires rendering it necessary to inform our correspondents and subscribers, without delay, an extra will be issued and forwarded by the first mail, so they can have all the benefits of an attentive correspondent without the expense of letter postage.

The first page each week will be devoted to such remarks as will best serve the interest of that class who are constantly receiving promiscuous Bank Notes.

The Typographical department will be conducted without reference to expense, and no pains spared to render this Reporter as perfect as possible.

TERMS

Mail subscribers, payable in all cases in advance, $3 00 per annum
Four subscribers clubbing together   10 00
Postmasters or others sending $12 for four subscribers will be put upon the subscription list gratis.
Single copies at the office 6¼ cents, 12 copies 50 cts. Office 25 Wall St.

T. THOMPSON.

N.B.—A few advertisements will be admitted under certain restrictions.

The name "T. Thompson" appearing in the foregoing advertisement is definitely a misprint and should have been "J. Thompson," the style which he apparently preferred to use and did use throughout his business career. His entrance into the publishing field was favorably received by the press, as indicated by the following announcements that subsequently appeared:

Bank Note Reporter.—Mr. J. Thompson, Exchange Broker, 52 Wall Street, publishes a very valuable "Bank Reporter." It came out yesterday, and is decidedly in favor of Captain Tyler's plan of finance. We recommend this periodical to every person who wants an accurate guide to the value of all sorts of bank note currency.[6]

*   *   *   *   *

Thompson's Bank Note Table.—The number for this week of this very valuable publication, will be published this morning at No. 52

[6] *New York Herald*, February 19, 1842.

The Reporters and Their Publishers

Wall Street. It contains a vast amount of information respecting broken banks' notes, Counterfeits, Exchanges, Specie &c., all compiled by Mr. Thompson, who is himself an active dealer in all these things.[7]

While the original advertisement refers to his reporter as a weekly, the issue of March 23, 1842, indicates that it was published on Wednesday and Saturday. It was then entitled *Thompson's Bank Note Reporter*. The cover page carries the following terms of subscription: Mail subscribers, payable in all cases in advance, Monthly, $1, per annum—Semi-monthly, $2, Weekly $3, Semi-Weekly, $5, Single copies 6¼ cts., loose or in wrappers ready to direct.—Four subscribers, clubbing together, for weekly, $10—Postmasters, or others, sending $12, for four subscribers, will be put upon the subscription list gratis—all letters to this office must be post-paid.

Thompson issued from time to time three other related publications (*see* pp. 142, 150, and 152) as supplements to his reporter. In one of these publications issued in 1848, an advertisement announces that the *Reporter* was then being issued at the following per annum rates: daily (except Sunday) at $12, weekly at $2, semi-monthly at $1, and monthly at 50¢. After having been a publisher for seven years, Thompson made this statement regarding his *Reporter*:

This work grows out of a desire to be *useful*, and the determination that while we *do* issue a reporter, it shall be, not merely *a* bank note reporter, but *The Bank Note Reporter;* and hence anything pertaining to bank notes or other species of money which can be serviceable to our subscribers and the trading community, we are determined to place before them.[8]

Sometime prior to 1849, the title changed to *The Bank Note & Commercial Reporter*, and a copy dated January 23, 1851, shows that it was then published semi-weekly. That same issue announced that the information contained therein was corrected by J. Thomp-

---

[7] *New York Journal of Commerce*, February 19, 1842.
[8] *The Autographical Counterfeit Detector*, 1849.

son, Stock and Exchange Broker of 64 Wall Street, and that it was published by Wm. W. Lee of 12 Spruce Street. In the issue of April 15, 1852, a claimed circulation of 50,000 was announced which had increased to 66,000 by October 16 of the same year. Prior to this date the *Reporter* appeared as a pamphlet about 11 inches by 7½ inches. The October 16, 1852, issue was increased in size to about 11½ inches by 9 inches. The issue of January 1, 1853, indicates that the *Reporter* was then published not oftener than weekly and the issue of June 1 of the same year shows a change of title to *Thompson's Bank Note and Commercial Reporter*. At that same date a circulation of 75,000 was announced which had increased to 80,000 by August 15, 1853. By March 1, 1855, Thompson's reporter had achieved a circulation of 100,000 which was by far the largest circulation claimed by any periodical of this type up to that time.

Thompson appears to have enjoyed a good reputation in most of his dealings, as evidenced by the following comments of a contemporary bank note engraver:

It has doubtless been observed that we have recognized and quoted as a standard work, the Bank Note and Commercial Reporter, edited by J. Thompson, Banker and Broker,—published by W. Lee. These gentlemen evidently take a lively interest in the dissemination of information, in regard to every thing connected with a sound and unadulterated currency. The main object of their journal is to describe Counterfeit Bank Bills, and to guard the public as far as possible against frauds of every kind in relation thereto.[9]

Thompson's reporter had a national reputation as a journal giving trustworthy information and several of his contemporaries confirm this statement. His bold denunciation of bad banking practices involved him in several lawsuits, one of which is referred to (in his reminiscences) in these words:

About 1838 Moses Y. Beach, having owned the *Sun* for several

---

[9] W. L. Ormsby, *A Description of the Present System of Bank Note Engraving*, New York: 1852, p. 63.

years, was organizing wildcat banks in New Jersey, Washington, etc. I exposed his nefarious schemes in my *Bank Note Reporter*. To get square with me he attacked me in the *Sun* in an outrageous way, calling me all sorts of hard names. My lawyers told me that he was liable for heavy damages and advised me to enter suit. I did so, and employed "Prince" John Van Buren, the brilliant son of Martin Van Buren, to make the closing speech at the trial. When the case went to the jury they gave me all I asked—$10,000—without leaving their seats.[10]

Thompson was proud of his reputation and standing and frequently impressed upon his subscribers his honest methods and policies. In his issue of August 15, 1853, is found this maxim:

> *We have No Sympathies to Influence*
> *No Favours to Ask—No Fears to Consult*

In our editorial character the above is our motto, and as we put it in type we impress it deeper in our heart.

We reproduce this motto, at this time, because we see that several of the Western Bank Note Reporters are denounced and condemned for quoting and puffing Shinplasters. We are too old to be trapped by fog-financiers. 'Tis our delight to crush them—'tis our sport to agonize them—'tis our duty to exterminate them.

We see them on their winding way.

We discover them tampering with the engravers—puffing their swindles, in advertisements—occasionally buying up an editor, (no allusion to long John), and often fastening upon green publishers of Bank Note Lists. We have felt the slimy skin of a Shinplaster Banker grasping us by the hand, but we much prefer a libel suit (no allusion to Geo. Smith) to any such contact.

Panic in Wall Street

In 1857, a panic came to Wall Street and the nation, and brought about a number of bank failures. On August 25, 1857, the Ohio Life Insurance and Trust Company of Cincinnati failed. This company whose currency enjoyed a wide circulation was incorporated in

---

[10] *The Bankers' Magazine*, etc., New York: June, 1891, p. 989.

1834 and for many years operated an agency at 45 Wall Street in New York City. This failure apparently caught Thompson unprepared and the following day his suspension was announced. The *New York Tribune* for August 26, 1857, announced: "This suspension is much to be regretted, and will cause considerable inconvenience at the West. Mr. Thompson has been for years the largest purchaser of uncurrent bank notes, and has acted largely as agent for interior banks."[11] As a result of his failure Thompson promptly turned over the publication of his reporter to Platt Adams who had been associated with him for several years. He announced that he would continue his connection with the paper in the editorial department.

THOMPSON UNDER CRITICISM

An account of one instance when Thompson was severely criticized by a rival publisher was found in the September 15, 1857, issue of *Lord's Detector and Bank Note Vignette Describer,* edited by Thomas R. Lord and published in Cincinnati. This tirade took much the same pattern as that followed by Thompson himself and other publishers from time to time. The article entitled "Thompsonian Banks" speaks for itself and read in part as follows:

Since the failure of John Thompson, the great New York propagandist of "wild-cat" money, these "lame ducks" have suddenly been thrown upon their own resources and bottoms for sustainment; and the consequences have been most disastrous both to the concerns themselves and those who were so unfortunate as to have any of this so-called money on hand. An immediate and simultaneous smashing up of these "Cats" was the result of Thompson's failure, showing most conclusively that all the vitality and life they possessed were derived simply from a quotation in the columns of the "Reporter." It is almost needless for us to inform our readers that Thompson was well paid by the owners of these "pets" for his kindness in taking them under his paternal care. Thompson's successor in the "Reporter" will, in all probability, attempt to throw himself into the saddle of his vanquished and "illustrious predecessors,"

[11] *American Banker*, June 15, 1936, Section Three, p. 35.

but, if we are not greatly mistaken, the people of the West have had enough of Eastern wild-cat money and bogus Counterfeit Detectors. In one point of view, at least, the failure of Thompson has done good, and that is, the whole of Eastern wild-cat bankers have now received a check on their nefarious designs that will "cripple them for life," but greatly redound to the benefit of community. His "Reporter" has now lost most of its subscribers through the last exposures of its proprietor, and with it has departed the power and prestige to do evil never-more.

Editor Lord then listed five banks situated in Rhode Island which he indicated have become "bereft of their paternal protector— 'Thompson's Reporter.' " He then goes on to say: "It makes no difference in what 'Reporter' you may see them favorably quoted and 'puffed,' do not be rash and retire to bed with any of their notes in your pockets." Continuing, he said, "Some of them [the five Rhode Island Banks] have had our 'mark' upon them for months past; and unless they give us better proof of their solvency than a mere quotation in the Ghost of Platt Adams'—'Thompson's Reporter'—we shall continue to give them the BENEFIT of our suspicions and circulation." He refers further to this situation in the following manner: "Thompson's failure, it seems, has embarrassed other banks which had allied their fortunes with those of their god-father; but to what extent has not transpired. Take our advice, and have nothing to do with Eastern money at the present time, except that which is known to be good and well secured."

One thing that Editor Lord failed to mention in his comments was that Thompson's financial difficulties were mainly due to the suspension (only three weeks before) of the Ohio Life Insurance and Trust Company whose main office was domiciled in Cincinnati where Lord's reporter was published.

The issue of May 1, 1858, then entitled *Thompson's Bank Note and Commercial Reporter,* shows it to have been "Edited by J. Thompson, and Corrected by Thompson Brothers, No. 2 Wall Street." The firm of Thompson Brothers no doubt comprised his two sons, Samuel Clark, then about twenty-four years old, and Frederick Ferris, about twenty-two years old.

Thompson's reporter continued to enjoy a good circulation and he no doubt re-established himself financially. His close familiarity with banks, and especially with the use and abuse of State bank notes, brought him to the conclusion that a national currency system was needed. In 1861, he urged upon President Lincoln and Secretary of the Treasury Chase the establishment of such a system.[12]

When the ten per cent tax on State bank notes became effective in 1866 in order to further the interests of national banks, the primary need for bank note reporters as such became unnecessary and Thompson's reporter became a bank directory in the modern sense. It has been in continuous existence to this day and now appears as the *American Banker,* the only daily banking newspaper.

LIBEL ACTION AGAINST THOMPSON

Thompson, as previously stated, was frequently involved in litigation, due to the nature of his business. Few cases, however, were carried to the higher courts, and as a result, records thereof are not found in official reports. One reported case referred to a libel action against him by the Shoe and Leather Bank. In July, 1862, at the Special Term of the New York Supreme Court, Thompson demurred to the complaint. In the written opinion the Court among other things stated:

> The defendant is the publisher of Thompson's Bank Note and Commercial Reporter, a paper having a large circulation among the inhabitants of the city and state of New York and other cities and states of the United States. He is charged in the complaint with having published in this paper several items manifestly calculated to affect the plaintiffs' credit as a banking institution.[13]

[12] *American Banker,* June 15, 1936, Section Three, pp. 35-36.
[13] The Shoe and Leather Bank *agt.* John Thompson, 23 How. Pr. 253, 254.

The demurrer was overruled. In the General Term of the Supreme Court for the First District in February, 1865, however, there was argued an appeal from the order overruling the demurrer filed in 1861. In the opinion rendered the following statements were made:

The plaintiffs, a banking corporation formed under the laws of the State of New York, brought this action to recover damages for a publication made by the defendant in a paper called "Thompson's Bank Note and Commercial Reporter," which stated that there were 50's and 100's of notes of the bank said to be counterfeits, and as the signatures on the genuine notes of the bank are engraved, the officers were in doubt as to which were good.

The complaint after setting out the above matters and the circulation of the paper, averred that divers neighbors and citizens to whom the innocence of the plaintiff was unknown, have since the publication, refused to receive the notes of the plaintiffs, and have refused to have any dealings or business transactions with the plaintiffs in their business of banking as they formerly had, to the great damage of the plaintiff.

The complaint also contained similar allegations as to another publication by the defendant, that the bank would not pay drafts upon it, and that he saw no reason why the bank may not at any time be closed by an injunction, with similar averments as to damage.

The defendant is the publisher of Thompson's Bank Note and Commercial Reporter, a paper having a large circulation among the inhabitants of the city and State of New York, and other cities and States of the United States. He is charged in the complaint with having published in this paper several items manifestly calculated to affect the plaintiff's credit as a banking institution. Among other items of intelligence contained in it are the following: "We would observe to those interested, that we see no reason why the Shoe and Leather Bank may not at any time be closed up by an injunction." "After promising to quote the Merchants' Bank at Trenton, I was informed that legal proceedings against the Shoe and Leather Bank were already under advisement."[14]

[14] The Shoe and Leather Bank *agt.* John Thompson, 18 Abb. Pr. 413, 415.

The decision on this appeal was that the demurrer had been properly overruled. On December 13, 1865, there was filed in the Supreme Court a consent and order of discontinuance in which attorneys for the plaintiff and the defendant agreed that the action be discontinued without costs to either party. Apparently Frederick F. and Samuel C. Thompson, sons of John, were involved in a similar action as a consent and order of discontinuance on their behalf was also filed on the same day.

The Thompsons As National Bankers

Shortly after the passage of The National Currency Act in 1863, The First National Bank of the City of New York (Charter No. 29) came into existence. While the name of John Thompson does not appear as one of the organizers, his two sons were original subscribers for a very substantial amount of the stock, and Samuel was its president for several years. Platt Adams, the publisher of Thompson's reporter for several years, and Charles Blondell, the publisher in 1867-1868, were also among the original subscribers to stock.

The National Currency Bank of New York was established in May, 1864, mainly as an agency for the redemption of national bank notes. While the name of John Thompson does not appear as one of the organizers, his two sons and his son-in-law, Francis G. Adams, were original subscribers for 97 per cent of the stock and Frederick F. Thompson was its president for several years.

In 1876, the Thompsons, having previously disposed of their interests in The First National Bank of the City of New York, decided to liquidate The National Currency Bank of New York, it not having been a profitable organization. In reporting this fact, a contemporary writer among other comments made the terse statement, "*Sic transit gloria*—Thompson No. 2." This bit of sarcasm on the part of that writer was no doubt an inference that the "glory" of the Thompsons in the banking business was about to pass away forever, they having disposed of their interests in The First National

Bank and being about to place The National Currency Bank in liquidation. This, however, was not the case; the *glory* of the Thompsons *did not pass.* In September, 1877, John Thompson then seventy-five years old, his son Samuel, his son-in-law Francis G. Adams, Lewis E. Ranson, a drug importer in New York City, and Isaac W. White, a dry goods merchant of Poughkeepsie, became the sole original shareholders and the first board of directors of The Chase National Bank of the City of New York. Samuel C. Thompson was that bank's first president and served in that capacity until his death in 1884, at which time his father, then about eighty-one years old, succeeded him. John Thompson served as president about two years and returned to the vice presidency when Henry W. Cannon became president.

John Thompson died on April 19, 1891, at the age of eighty-eight, after a varied and interesting career, his life having spanned a most important period in American history. He was an outstanding personality in his field and without doubt the most conservative and most prominent of all of the publishers of bank note reporters. Hoyt Sherman, a contemporary of John Thompson and previously referred to as a prominent banker in Iowa, cited Thompson's reporter as "the standard authority." While John Thompson was at times subjected to a certain amount of criticism, as were practically all such publishers, there were more favorable comments by contemporary writers with respect to him than of any other publisher. He was an American of the highest type and his full and abundant life was one of outstanding service to the banking fraternity.

Charles — McIntyre — Leonori — Taylor

Early in 1840, Edmund Charles and Archibald McIntyre, under the firm name of Charles, McIntyre & Co., began the weekly publication of *New-York Telegraph, M'Intyre's Gazette and General Advertiser.* This was a four page edition about the size of our present day tabloid newspapers. It appears to have been the first of a series of publications of this type which continued for about twenty years under the aegis of several more or less connected proprietorships. In the issue of May 6, 1840, this statement is found regarding this reporter: "It has extensive circulation throughout the United States and Canada." The October 15, 1840, issue shows that the title had been changed to *New-York Telegraph, McIntyre's Bank Note List and Prices Current*. The publishers were at that time exchange and commission brokers with offices at 208 Broadway, New York City.

McIntyre, the more prominent member of this firm, was for several years prior to entering the publication field a member of the firm of Yates and McIntyre who managed lotteries in the State of New York. John B. Yates of this firm was a resident of Chittenango, New York. Archibald McIntyre was born in Scotland and came to this country when about two years old with his parents who settled first in Haverstraw, New York, and moved later to Broadalbin, New York. He was in the New York State Legislature from 1799 to 1801, appointed Deputy Secretary of State of New York in October, 1801, and in March, 1806, he became State Comptroller of New York, in which position he served until February, 1821. In 1823, he served in the New York State Senate.[15]

The State Comptroller had supervision over lotteries, and it was no doubt due to this circumstance that McIntyre later became actively engaged in managing lotteries. His firm managed the New York Literature Lottery, a portion of the proceeds of which was granted to Union College of Schenectady, as a result of which their firm was involved in extended litigation.

After the *New-York Telegraph, McIntyre's Bank Note List and Prices Current* had been in existence about two years, an announcement was made that "Chas. McIntyre & Co., 208 Broadway, have just issued the first number of a Bank Note List which will con-

---

[15] A sermon by William B. Sprague, D.D., Minister of the Second Presbyterian Congregation, Albany, New York, Sunday, May 9, 1858, on occasion of the death of Hon. Archibald McIntyre.

tinue weekly." [16] Later that same year there came into existence *The New York Bank Note List, Counterfeit Detector, Wholesale Prices Current, and General Banking Statistic*, with Edmund Charles & Son as publishers, "successors to Charles, McIntyre & Co." The February 15, 1843, issue of this publication is a small pamphlet of thirty-two pages, containing the information usually found in periodicals of this type. It was published semi-monthly at two dollars per annum, from their office at 12 (now 23) Wall Street. It was at this same address that John Thompson, the prominent publisher of a bank note reporter, established himself in 1832. This publication continued for several years and in 1847 it was known as *Edmund Charles & Son's New York Bank Note List, Counterfeit Detector, Wholesale Prices Current and Weekly Journal of Financial News.* The issue of March 20, 1847, was in pamphlet form, of sixteen pages, and then published weekly at two dollars per annum from 37 Wall Street.

Competition between publishers of bank note reporters was quite keen and they did not hesitate to print critical comments of their competitors, some of which bordered on libelous statements. The following interesting reference to Charles and McIntyre was found in a contemporary reporter:

Charles & Son! alias *McIntire & Co.*

Since our last publication we have received many letters from different parts of the Union, which come from parties who have been victimized, or rather swindled by the individuals whose names are at the head of this article. We are apprised of what we before knew—that they are at the head of an enormous lottery, or rather gambling business, and the system they have adopted heretofore to make their schemes known is, to send them far and near under the title of "New York Commercial Circular," and the name of "Charles, McIntire & Co." [17]

[16] *New York Express*, February 17, 1842.
[17] *Mearson's United States Bank Note Reporter*, June 5, 1847.

About December, 1846, *Taylor's United States Money Reporter and Gold and Silver Coin Examiner* began its existence. Its sponsor, S. Taylor, conducted a specie and exchange office at 90 Broadway in March, 1847, and a few months later operated as S. Taylor & Co., at Wall and Broad Streets. In December of the same year George DeMott was the publisher at the foregoing address. In 1849, C. S. Sloane, an exchange broker at 23 Wall Street, was found to be the publisher of this reporter.

About 1850, the two aforementioned reporters appear to have been succeeded by *Charles & Leonori's New York Bank Note List, Counterfeit Detector, Wholesale Prices Current, and Commercial Journal.* The August 23, 1851, issue of this journal is a small pamphlet of twenty-four pages and it was published every Saturday morning at two dollars per annum. The firm at that time consisted of Edmund Charles and Lewis J. Leonori, and they were located at 35 Wall Street. About 1852, Charles appears to have retired from the firm and this publication continued until late in 1856 as *Leonori's New York Bank Note Reporter, Counterfeit Detector & Wholesale Prices Current.* At that time it claimed a circulation of 45,000 copies.

Late in 1856 or early in 1857, a "new" reporter made its appearance. Its masthead, format and title was identical with that of the aforementioned except that the name "Leonori" had been omitted. The publisher, H. S. Taylor, was a printer located at 61 Beekman Street. His name is listed in *Trow's New York Directory* for May 1, 1859, as the publisher of a Bank & Commercial Reporter at 208 Broadway. He is not listed after that date. This publication appears to have been the last of a continuous succession of more or less closely related publications of this type over a period of about twenty years.

Mahlon Day

The pioneer in this field of periodicals appears quite definitely to have been Mahlon Day, a printer, bookseller, and publisher of children's books whose address at different times is given as 372, 374, and 376 Pearl Street in New York City. Day was born August 27, 1790, at Morristown, New Jersey, and was established in the printing business in New York City as early as 1815.[18]

On the first page of his September 6, 1837, reporter, which was known at that time as *Day's New York Bank Note List, Counterfeit Detector & Price Current,* the following statement appears: "Established in 1819, Being the oldest paper of the kind." There is little question as to the correctness of the statement that his detector was *the oldest paper of the kind.* It is, however, quite uncertain that he began the publication of a bank note reporter, as such, as early as 1819. On February 21, 1815, Mahlon Day, in association with one Charles Turner, began the publication of a semi-weekly known as *New-York Shipping and Commercial List.* This paper contained, among other information, prices of stocks, prices current, notices of ship arrivals, importations, and rates of insurance. The issue of July 18, 1817, contains a table entitled "Bank Note Exchange." This table includes a list of banks whose notes were, at that time, received at par in New York City, together with a list of banks whose notes were not received on deposit by banks in New York City. It also included a list of banks located outside New York City, together with rates of discount at which their bank notes would be purchased. In subsequent issues at certain intervals bank note tables continued to be published.

In the issue of this publication for September 10, 1819, an announcement was made that Mahlon Day was withdrawing from the firm of Day and Turner and that he would continue the printing and stationery business on his own account. The announcement also stated that C. Turner and Company would continue publication of the bank note table in the *New-York Shipping and Commercial List.*

[18] Harry B. Weiss, "Mahlon Day," *Bulletin of The New York Public Library,* XLV (December, 1941), p. 1007.

Among the many publications of Day was a miniature almanac which he issued annually for many years. The earliest almanac found was that of 1823 under the title *Day's New-York Miniature Almanac*. In addition to the usual information found in most almanacs, it contains one page of very brief information pertaining to discount rates on bank notes and two pages of brief information regarding counterfeit and spurious notes. It *was* a miniature almanac, being but 3½ by 2 inches in size, and when the size of the page is visualized, one can well understand that the information contained on one page would necessarily be very brief. His almanacs for the years 1824 and 1825 contain information regarding bank notes similar to that found in the 1823 issue. His almanacs, however, for the years 1826 and 1827 have one page devoted to the discount rate on bank notes and no information regarding counterfeit notes. In the issue of 1828, the same size as his almanac for 1823, the information regarding bank notes and counterfeits was omitted. His almanacs for the years 1829, 1830 and 1831 carry a short notice to the effect that Day is the publisher of "the bank note list and counterfeit detector." The fact that information regarding counterfeits was omitted from the 1826 almanac might lead to the inference that information of this sort was brought to the attention of the public by Day in some other manner. The 1848 almanac is numbered 30, which would indicate that the annual series may have started in 1819.[19] This may have some connection with Day's statement that his "detec*ter*" was established in 1819. Further light as to the date his reporter first appeared may be gathered from the following notice:

Published this day, the *New York Bank Note List and Counterfeit Detecter*, shewing the value of Bank Notes in New York and a complete list of counterfeit bills in circulation throughout the United States —for sale at the bookstore of

MAHLON DAY,
376 Pearl Street.

[19] Harry B. Weiss, *op. cit.*, p. 1012.

N.B.—Persons residing out of the city, can have the Detecter furnished them for one year, by forwarding two dollars in advance.[20]

The earliest issue discovered is dated August 16, 1830, at which time it was known as *Day's New-York Bank Note List, Counterfeit Detecter and Price Current*. Upon the title-page the following statement is found: "Entered according to an Act of Congress the 30th day of October, 1826, by Mahlon Day, of the State of New York." It will be noted that this date precedes by only two months the date of the aforementioned advertisement.

It seems appropriate to present a rather detailed description of the contents of Day's detector for August 16, 1830, it being the earliest issue found of any periodical of this type. It is a folio of four pages about 20 by 13 inches in size, of attractive appearance and typography. The first page consists of five columns of the usual newspaper size and includes the names of approximately 500 banks in the various States of the Union at that time, together with a quotation in most cases of the discount rate at which notes of those banks could be disposed of in New York City. This information was furnished by John T. Smith & Co., exchange brokers at 25 (now 42) Wall Street, which firm continued for many years to furnish Day with similar quotations. There is a short table of exchange for buying and selling bills of exchange above and below par. There is also a list of about 50 banks and insurance companies in New York City "exhibiting the duration of their Charters, Capitals, par amount of Shares, times of paying Dividends, Discount Days, Current Price of Stock, &c." The second and third pages are devoted to "A List of Counterfeit Bills, of Altered Notes and those with Spurious Signers, throughout the U. States." The last page includes late information of counterfeits, a rather complete list of New York wholesale prices current, a list of incorporated banks in New York State outside of New York City, a list of "broken" banks, rates of postage, list of counterfeit coins, a table of distances between sev-

[20] *New-York Advertiser*, December 29, 1826.

John S. Dye

In 1850, John S. Dye appears to have sponsored the publication in Cincinnati of *Dye's Counterfeit Detector and Universal Bank Note Gazetteer*. It was a small pamphlet about 8½ by 5½ inches in size. One issue dated 1850 (no month) was said to contain "correct rules by which spurious notes may be detected at a glance, also a list of all the fraudulent and broken banks and altered notes; and a list of all the solvent banks, with rates of discount." Another edition of this same periodical bears a Philadelphia imprint, under the same date, and was published in that city by Joseph Arnold. Their contents were by no means as complete as those found in other bank note reporters of that period. Dye in later years was said to be ". . . a recognized authority on the paper and precious currencies of the world. . . ." [24] In 1852, the title appears to have been changed to *Dye's Bank Mirror and Illustrated Counterfeit Detector*.[25]

Sometime within the next two years Dye moved to New York City and *Dye's Bank Mirror*, then published at 172 Broadway (cor. Maiden Lane), was described in this manner: "The Mirror is semi-monthly and contains a description of all new Counterfeits, Banks, &c., and is embellished with engraved descriptions of every dangerous Counterfeit, forming altogether the cheapest means of ascertaining all news connected with Banks, &c., in the country." [26]

The following advertisement gave a detailed account of one of Dye's publications, and while it makes no mention of the title, it was without much doubt a description of his *Bank Mirror:*

> *The Most Useful, Most Perfect, Most Concise*
> Published weekly. $1.00 per annum.

Greatest Discovery of the Present Century for Detecting Counterfeit Bank Notes.

[24] *Dye's Coin Encyclopaedia*, Philadelphia: 1883.
[25] W. L. Ormsby, *A Description of the Present System of Bank Note Engraving*, New York: 1852, p. 41.
[26] *Dye's Bank Note Plate Delineator*, New York: 1855.

Describing every genuine bill in existence, and exhibiting at a glance every counterfeit in circulation!

Arranged so admirably, that reference is easy, and detection instantaneous.

No index to examine! No pages to hunt up! But so simplified and arranged that the Merchant Banker and Business Man can see all at a glance.

It has taken years to make perfect this Great Discovery. The urgent need for such a work has long been felt by Commercial men. It has been published to supply the call for such a preventive, and needs but to be known to be universally patronized. It does more than has ever been attempted by man. It describes every Bank Note in three different languages, English, French and German.

The paper will be about 28 by 24 inches, and will contain the most perfect bank note list published, together with the rate of discount. Also a list of all the private bankers in America.[27]

Some years later the title of Dye's detector was changed to *Dye's Government Counterfeit Detector* and the office of publication was moved to Philadelphia. In 1879, he was located at 1338 Chestnut Street, "Opposite the United States Mint." At that time he styled himself as a "Treasury Expert." The later named publication continued for many years after the end of the State bank note era.

John S. Dye was also the publisher of *Dye's Wall Street Broker*, which appeared as early as 1847, and he also issued a publication entitled *Bank Bulletin*, a daily which began its existence about 1855.[28]

FREDERICH GERHARD

From about 1856 to 1867, one Frederich Gerhard published the *German Bank Note Reporter* in New York City. In the earlier years it was published semi-monthly, and during the last five or six years of its existence it was published weekly. Gerhard was located at several downtown addresses in the following chronological order:

[27] *The Falls City Register* (Paterson, New Jersey), March 11, 1857.
[28] J. H. French, *Gazetteer of the State of New York*, Syracuse: 1860, pp. 443-444.

133, 58, and 81 Nassau Street, 197 William Street, and 15 Dey Street.

Notwithstanding the fact that this reporter was published over a period of more than ten years, with total individual issues in excess of 350, no copies were discovered.

Gwynne & Day — H. J. Messenger

About 1854, John A. Gwynne and Clarence S. Day established a banking and brokerage business in New York City under the firm name of Gwynne & Day. In the early part of 1858, they appear to have sponsored the monthly publication of *The Bank Note Register and Detector of Counterfeits*. This was a small pamphlet with subscription rates at fifty cents per annum to monthly subscribers and $2.50 per annum to weekly subscribers. About two years later the title was changed to *Metropolitan Bank Note Reporter* and some years later to *Metropolitan National Bank Note Reporter*. It appears to have continued under the direction of Messrs. Gwynne & Day until about 1865 when H. J. Messenger, a banker at 139 Broadway, became the publisher.

The issue of February 17, 1866 (Vol. 8, No. 43, Whole Number 407) is a small pamphlet of forty pages and circulated then at $3.50 per annum to weekly subscribers. In this issue is found the following statement: "The quotations in the body of the Reporter for New York State, New England, and New Jersey, are furnished by the Metropolitan Bank, and the rates at which that institution credits such funds to account of its regular dealers."

Messenger was quite active as an up-State (New York) private banker and operated as such at various times at Canandaigua, Canton, Cortland, Geneva, Herkimer, and Marathon. This periodical appears to have been published until about 1868, at which time Messenger was reported as having been "unable to meet payments."[29]

[29] *The Bankers' Magazine*, etc., New York: June, 1868, p. 987.

The Hodges

John Tyler Hodges and Daniel Milton Hodges, brothers, and Edward Milton Hodges, a son of Daniel, were prominent publishers of a bank note reporter from about 1856 to 1866. About 1855, John was engaged as a banker at Broadway, corner of Canal Street, and Daniel as a broker at 114 Grand Street.[30] Entirely reliable information is not available for the first few years of their venture in the publishing field. The volume numbers on their reporter in later years indicate that the first issue appeared about 1856. About 1857, a weekly entitled *Journal of Finance & Bank Reporter* was published by Monroe & Hodges.[31] That firm consisted of James Monroe and J. Tyler Hodges and was located at 271 Broadway. In 1859, J. T. Hodges was found to be the proprietor of the *Journal of Finance & Bank Reporter* and J. Monroe as the proprietor of the *Journal of Finance* at 4 Wall Street.[32]

The issue of January 1, 1861, appeared as *Hodges' Journal of Finance and Bank Note Reporter* with Daniel M. Hodges as editor and proprietor, with a claimed circulation of 103,000. Daniel died in January, 1862, at which time his son Edward, then about twenty-five years old, took over the publication which he continued until the latter part of 1865. The January 1, 1866, issue, then under the editorship of James N. Phelps, and with the title changed to *National Journal of Finance and Hodges' Bank Note Reporter,* carried a notice which read in part as follows:

> The radical change ... and the general absorption of State by National Banks, having in a great measure curtailed the field of operations for counterfeiters, as well as both the demand and necessity for a weekly counterfeit detector we have come to the conclusion ... to discontinue for the present the weekly publication of the Bank Note Reporter ... and to issue in its stead a first-class financial and commercial newspaper ... The National Journal of Finance. ...

[30] *Trow's New York Directory,* 1854-1855.
[31] *Wilson's* (New York) *Directory,* 1857-1858.
[32] *Trow's New York Directory,* May 1, 1859.

The National Journal of Finance will be forwarded regularly to the weekly subscribers of the Reporter ... "Hodges' Journal of Finance and Bank Note Reporter" will be issued hereafter on the first of every month; ....

This reporter was issued in good form and style and can be classed among the better publications of this type. The publishers were quite frank in expressing their opinion as to the condition of the banks and their January 1, 1861, issue contains a column headed "THROWN OUT!" followed by the statement "The notes of the following banks are thrown out by the brokers:—" There are then listed the names of thirty-seven banks located in twelve different States and Canada. This same issue contains a column headed "Our present list of Equivocal and Doubtful Banks, whose notes should be refused," which contains the names of thirty-seven banks in fifteen States, Canada, and the District of Columbia.

During the period in which their reporter was issued, the Hodges' from time to time also published *Hodges' New Bank Note Safe-Guard, Hodges' Genuine Notes of America,* and *Hodges' Coin Chart Manual.* In 1861, their yearly subscription rates for the reporter, including the Safe-Guard (with Monthly Supplements) and the Coin Chart Manual, were: weekly $4.00, semi-monthly $3.00 and monthly $2.50. Rates for the reporter for one year including *Hodges' Genuine Notes of America* and *Hodges' Coin Chart Manual* were: weekly $2.50, semi-monthly $1.50 and monthly $1.00. Hodges' reporter is not listed in *Trow's New York Directory* for 1866-1867, which would appear to indicate that publication ceased in 1866.

L. S. LAWRENCE & CO.

About 1858, L. S. Lawrence & Co., bankers and brokers at 164 Nassau Street, were proprietors of a publication known as *L. S. Lawrence & Cos.' Bank Note List.* Samuel French was the publisher. The March 3, 1858, issue was in pamphlet form and consisted of thirty-two pages. It was issued weekly in New York and a New

England Edition was issued semi-monthly in Boston. It does not appear to have existed more than two years.

GEORGE MEARSON

About May, 1846, George Mearson of 48 Gold Street, New York City, began the publication of *Mearson's United States Bank Note Reporter*. It was a weekly in pamphlet form and sold for three cents a copy. In the June 5, 1847, issue (the only copy found), it claimed to have "a guaranteed circulation" of 8,000 copies weekly. Mearson operated a print shop where as he stated he could "undertake book work of every description and also stereotyping."

This reporter contains the usual list of banks together with the rate of discount on their notes and a description of outstanding counterfeits. Information therein was corrected weekly by A. Nicholas, an exchange broker located at 52 Wall Street. Nicholas, some years later, published a bank note reporter under his own name. Mearson's reporter does not appear to have continued publication after 1849.

L. MENDELSON

About July, 1864, L. Mendelson of 76 Nassau Street, New York City, began the publication of the *National Bank Note Reporter*. This was a weekly in pamphlet form at $5 per annum to weekly subscribers, $3 to semi-monthly subscribers and $1.50 to monthly subscribers. It contained a list of the National banks, State banks, and "retired" banks. The issue of July 1, 1866, consisting of forty-eight pages, in addition to the foregoing information contained stock quotations, financial news and a few advertisements. In December of the same year the name appears as *The National Bank Note Reporter and Financial Gazette*. The 1869-1870 New York City Directory indicates that A. Cohn was the publisher at that time. In June, 1876, when this reporter was edited by D. F. June, it was merged with *Thompson's Bank Note Reporter*.[33]

---

[33] *The American Banker*, June 15, 1936, Section Three, p. 38.

E. Morrison and Company

The Exporter and Banking Circular, a large folio of four pages, began publication about December, 1848, under the proprietorship of E. Morrison at 29 Wall Street, New York City. He was probably a member of the firm of E. Morrison and Company who were the publishers for a while of Sylvester's reporter. This circular, published weekly, contained three pages with the usual information with respect to rates of discount and description of counterfeits, while the last page was devoted almost entirely to advertisements of several lottery schemes being conducted mainly in Delaware and Virginia. Morrison was a dealer in uncurrent bank notes and offered for sale the various lottery tickets advertised in his paper.

Only one copy of this circular was found and there is no indication that its existence was very extended. In 1858, Morrison conducted an exchange, banking, and collection office at 51 William Street.

Anastasius Nicholas — Nicholas, Bowen & Co.

Anastasius Nicholas, an exchange broker, located at various times at 52, 68, 70, 74, and 90 Wall Street, sponsored the publication of *Nicholas' New York and Chicago Bank Note Reporter,* a weekly at $2.50 per annum. The earliest number found is dated January 18, 1862, Volume 7, Whole Number 324, which appears to indicate that this periodical began its existence about October, 1855. The issue referred to, in pamphlet form, consists of thirty-two pages, with the information therein having been corrected by A. Nicholas & Co., 90 Wall Street. The 1866-1867 and 1867-1868 New York directories indicate that Nicholas, Bowen & Co. were the publishers at that time. *Trow's New York Directory* for 1857-1858 lists A. Nicholas of 70 Wall Street as the publisher of "Bank Note List and Insurance Reporter." That may have been an early title of this publication. While "Chicago" is incorporated in the title of this reporter, it does not appear to have been published in that city at any time.

Nicholas' reporter appears to have been published weekly for about twelve years, a total of more than six hundred individual issues. After an exhaustive search in libraries and historical societies throughout the country, only four issues of this reporter were found. One in 1862, referred to above, one in 1863, and two in 1864. This clearly illustrates the ephemeral nature of these publications.

Sylvester J. Sylvester

One of the more important bank note reporters in New York City and the second to be published regularly was that sponsored by Sylvester J. Sylvester who began business about 1825. One of his earliest activities, as was that of several other publishers of bank note reporters, was the operation of a lottery and exchange office at 130 Broadway, where he was located for more than twenty years. In an early newspaper advertisement his establishment and address was referred to as "The Mint, Sylvester's, 130 Broadway." At that time his principal activity was the sale of lottery tickets, and in this same advertisement the public was urged to "call at once at Sylvester's Mint and large riches will be bestowed upon you with a bounteous hand." The advertisement also indicated that he purchased notes of broken banks.[34]

S. J. Sylvester appears to have begun the publication of his reporter about April, 1830. The earliest issue found, dated December 2, 1830 (No. 34), is entitled merely *Sylvester's Reporter*. It was a folio in form and quarto in size and described itself as being a weekly report of lotteries, bank notes, broken banks, and stock. The subscription rate was $1.50 per annum. This same issue indicates further that "The Reporter will give a correct list of Yates & McIntyre's Lottery Schemes and the official drawings of lotteries; also the value of Uncurrent Bank Notes—Broken Bank Bills—Gold—Silver—Bills of Exchange, Stocks, Shares, etc., etc." The next issue discovered is dated February 3, 1831 (Vol. 1, 2d. Series, No. 4), upon

[34] *New York Gazette & General Advertiser*, December 27, 1826.

which the title appears as *Sylvester's Reporter and Counterfeit Detector*. This issue, somewhat larger in size than the first, was at that time published every Thursday evening. The issue of March 24, 1831, also a folio, is about the same size as our present day tabloid newspaper. The issue of June 22, 1831, entitled *Sylvester's Reporter, Counterfeit Detector and New York Price Current*, was then published every Wednesday evening. The title on the issue of October 3, 1832 (Vol. III, 3d Ser., No. 38), appears as *Sylvester's Reporter, Counterfeit Detector, New York Price Current and General Advertiser*.

This reporter had the unique distinction of having been printed during a part of its existence by the eminent American journalist and statesman, Horace Greeley. In January, 1833, when Greeley was but twenty-two years of age and only two years after he arrived in New York City, he formed a partnership with Francis V. Story, a fellow-workman. One of their earliest ventures was the printing of *The Morning Post* which lasted less than three weeks. Greeley in his autobiography stated that his friend Story was acquainted with S. J. Sylvester, then a leading broker and seller of lottery tickets, who issued a weekly "Bank-Note Reporter," largely devoted to the advertising of his own business, who offered their partnership the job of printing that paper.[35] Greeley did not state how long their firm continued to print this reporter.

Shortly after Messrs. Greeley & Story undertook the printing of this reporter it appears to have entered an era of prosperity, and the issue of August 29, 1833 (Vol. IV, No. 41), indicates that the subscription rates had been increased to $2.50 per annum. This prosperity no doubt continued and the issue of December 25, 1837 (Vol. IX, No. 5), under the same title was published every Monday afternoon at the subscription rate of $3.00 per annum.

About 1838, a rival reporter, under a similar title, made its appearance and Sylvester in his issue for October 1, 1838, caused the following notice to be inserted:

[35] Horace Greeley, *Recollections of a Busy Life*, New York: 1872, p. 91.

S. J. Sylvester's Reporter.—A paper having lately appeared in this city under the title of "Sylvester's New Reporter," I deem it advisable, in order to prevent my friends and the public from being deceived thereby, to state that the name of my paper remains unchanged, and I am still at 130 Broadway, where I have been for thirteen years past— and of course have not removed therefrom.

The issue of August 12, 1839 (Vol. X, No. 38), indicates that this reporter was still published every Monday afternoon on what he then described as "a large imperial sheet." The subscription rate in November, 1848, had been reduced to $2 per annum and the reporter, still a large folio, continued to be published every Monday afternoon. It was then described as "containing a full and accurate list of all counterfeits in circulation.—Broken Banks and all the Fraudulent Institutions—Bank Note Table; comprising all the solvent banks in the Union, with the value of their notes in this city."

The latest number found is dated September 24, 1849, at which time it was published by E. Morrison and Company who were then located at 47 Wall Street, which location had previously been that of S. J. Sylvester.

E. J. Sylvester & Co.

About 1838, E. J. Sylvester & Co., who operated a lottery and exchange office at 156 Broadway, began publishing *Sylvester's New Reporter, Counterfeit Detector, Bank Note Table and New York Prices Current*. This publication had no connection whatsoever with that sponsored by S. J. Sylvester who was located at 130 Broadway. The issue of February 5, 1840, was a sixteen page pamphlet while the issue of June 23, 1840, consisted of a large sheet folded so as to make four pages. Its period of existence covered about three years.

Boston

Notwithstanding the prominence of Boston in the early history of this country only two bank note reporters of real importance appear to have been published in that city. There is evidence, however, that reporters published in other places circulated in Boston.

Clark

About January, 1838, *Clark's New-England Bank Note List and Counterfeit Bill Detector* made its appearance in Boston. In 1845, it was known as *Clark's New-England Bank Note List*. It was printed and published by J. N. Bang and corrected by J. W. Clark & Co., stock and exchange brokers of Boston. It was a monthly publication in pamphlet form and subscription rates were $1.50 per annum. Copies of this reporter were found bearing various dates from March, 1838, to November, 1846. No information was found that indicated when this reporter ceased publication.

Willis

October, 1843, is the month and year in which *Willis & Co.'s Bank Note List and Counterfeit Detecter* made its appearance in Boston. It was issued monthly in pamphlet form by Thomas Groom & Co., stationers, edited by Willis & Co., stock, exchange, and money brokers, and printed by Dickinson & Co. Subscription rates were $1.50 per annum.

The publishers announced in the issue of April, 1844, that:

> It will be their aim to give to the community, in a concise and tangible form, every information relative to the standing of the several Banking Institutions throughout the United States and the adjacent British Provinces; a description of their issue, rates of discount, and the names of their Presidents and Cashiers, enabling any one to detect at a glance the Counterfeit, Spurious, Mutilated or Altered Bank Note. Annexed to which will be a Table of the Value of Gold and Silver Coins; the Rates of Exchange and Discounts, with a complete list of the Market Value of Bank, Insurance, Government, State and other Stocks and such other information relative to Monetary affairs as shall be useful to every man of business.

In October, 1845, the publishers announced: "To those who will now commence with us, we inform them that we are just two years old; we started with an edition of 800, and now print 2000 copies monthly; ...." This reporter was published at least until September, 1854. Its discontinuance was due, no doubt, to financial difficulties of its publishers, as evidenced by the following notice: "In July 1854—Willis & Co., Bankers—Boston—were forced to suspend—due to the great pressure that prevailed at that time in the stock and monetary affairs of the country." [36]

CLAPP, FULLER & BROWNE

The outside cover page only of *Clapp, Fuller & Browne's Bank Note Reporter and Counterfeit Detecter* for March, 1859, was found.[37] It was published monthly by Thomas Groom & Co., of Boston, who had been the publishers of Willis & Co.'s reporter. This cover page is of the same format as that of Willis & Co.'s detector, and there is every reason to believe that it was a continuation of that publication. No information was obtained as to its period of existence, although one copy dated December, 1861, is known to exist. The directories for the City of Boston from 1846 to 1866 do not list any of the detectors published in Boston, nor any other publications of this type, and definite dates as to when those reporters ceased publication were not established.

LAWRENCE

There was a New England Edition of *L. S. Lawrence & Co.'s Bank Note List*, which publication appears to have had a short career in New York as well as in Boston. In the New York Edition of that periodical for March, 1858, under the caption "Opinions of the Press," the following article is quoted from the *Boston Daily Traveller* (no date):

[36] *The Bankers' Magazine*, etc., New York: August, 1854, p. 154.
[37] *Landauer Trade Cards*, Vol. 2, The New-York Historical Society.

L. S. Lawrence & Co.'s New York and New England Bank Note List for January has just been issued by Mr. W. F. Davis, 25 State Street. Mr. Davis is well known as a most skilful detector of counterfeit or altered notes. An experience of many years, commenced in the foreign money department of the Suffolk Bank, and continued, of late years, in one of the largest banking and exchange offices in State Street, has given him such an expertness that it would be a marvellous thing for a spurious note, of any description, to pass beneath his lynx-eyed gaze without detection. Mr. Davis will be the New England editor and publisher of the Detector, which will contain a large amount of useful and valuable matter to banking institutions—and, in fact, to every merchant and trader, none of whom should be without a Detector on their counters. The Detector is issued Semi-monthly, at 8 cents a copy, or $1.50 per annum.

BICKNELL'S BOSTON EDITION

In 1833, John J. Spear, a broker at 15 Exchange Street, Boston, published what might be termed a Boston edition of *Bicknell's* (Philadelphia) *Counterfeit Detector and Bank Note List.* The only copy found has on the outside cover page the year of publication, 1833, the title, name, and address of the publisher, together with the statement that it was "Published every six weeks, or eight numbers per annum." The inside cover page is the same as that of the edition published in Philadelphia. The issue found is dated May, 1833 (No. 2 of Volume I). From this it would appear that Spear in Boston obtained a supply of Bicknell's detector as printed in Philadelphia and merely added to it an outside cover page as a sort of "Boston Edition." No information was obtained as to the period of time covered by this edition.

BUFFALO

Under date of November 18, 1858, the *Bank Note Register and Counterfeit Detector*, a weekly, appeared in Buffalo, New York. Edward L. Lee was publisher and John R. Lee, the editor. Edward L. Lee was a banker and broker doing business at 11 Exchange

The Reporters and Their Publishers 115

Street, Buffalo, and John R. Lee was his cashier. This reporter was issued in pamphlet form and bears a striking resemblance to *The Bank Note Register and Detector of Counterfeits,* published by Gwynne & Day, Bankers, in New York City at the same time.

The following excerpt is taken from the prospectus which appeared in the first issue:

> We do not assume that our city has been, or is, suffering for the want of a work of the kind we have taken in hand, but we do claim that all the information required by our business community on the subject of Currency, Banking, &c., can be furnished at home; and the paper merchant, the printer, and others in our midst, become the recipients of the large patronage now bestowed on works of a similar character published elsewhere. Our claim will be to faithfully chronicle passing events coming within the scope of our paper; to speak of things as we find them without fear or favor, and, in all respects, to serve the interests of our patrons as we shall from time to time have opportunity.

This same issue also contains an announcement that the register is corrected in New York by E. Morrison, Esq., Banker; in Boston by Messrs. Clapp, Fuller & Browne, Bankers; in Cincinnati by Messrs. Geo. S. Wright & Co., Bankers; and in Chicago by F. Granger Adams, Esq., Banker. With the exception of Messrs. Geo. S. Wright & Co., the others named were also at various times publishers of periodicals of this type.

With the issue of January 13, 1859 (No. 9), the name was changed to *Lee's Bank Note Register and Counterfeit Detecter* under which title it continued until March 3, 1859 (No. 16). The issue of March 14, 1859 (No. 17) appears as *Bank Note Register and Counterfeit Detecter* under which title it continued at least until November 11, 1859 (No. 52). This register designated by the publisher as a "weekly" was dated anywhere from three to eleven days apart.

The fifty-two numbers of this register may be found in two volumes in the library of the Buffalo Historical Society. On the inside cover of one of the volumes appears the statement "From John R. Lee, Nov. 5, 1866." This was no doubt the editor's own personal file. It probably constitutes a complete file of this register, and appears to have been the only one that was ever published in Buffalo.

CHARLESTON

In 1854, *Monroe's Southern Banker* was published in Charleston, South Carolina. An account of its inception was found in the following editorial:

We have received the first number of this most necessary counterfeit detector and Commercial Reporter. A work of this kind has been long needed at the South, and we are pleased to see that Mr. Monroe has at once placed it on an equality with any of the old Northern publications. Our space this week will not allow us to enter into the details of its merits, but we would advise every merchant, planter and mechanic in our District to take it at once. Published monthly at Charleston, by J. Monroe, price $2 per annum.[38]

No further information was found with respect to this publication, or its period of existence.

CHICAGO

The present site of Chicago, upon which Fort Dearborn was established in 1804, was on an important portage route, used by the French in the earlier days. When Cook County was organized in 1831, Chicago was a small village which incorporated as a city in 1837. Its first banking institution, as such, was a branch of the State Bank of Illinois (*Second*) which came into existence in December, 1835. The Bank of Illinois, the first bank to receive a charter in what is now the State of Illinois, was incorporated in 1816 and established business at Shawneetown on the Ohio River in the extreme southern part of the State.

[38] *Laurensville Herald* (Laurens, South Carolina), May 5, 1834.

Sheldon—Adams

About June, 1853, when there were then less than ten banks doing business in Chicago, the first bank note reporter in that locality appears to have made its debut. It was in pamphlet form and quite similar in appearance to many others that were in circulation in several other places at that time. It was then known as *Sheldon's North American Bank Note Detector and Commercial Reporter,* and was published semi-weekly, weekly, semi-monthly, and monthly at the respective rates of $4, $2, $1.50, and $1 per annum. It was described as containing a list of all the broken, counterfeit and uncurrent bank notes in North America; review of the commercial markets; wholesale prices current; financial review; statistics; rates of discount of uncurrent money; foreign exports and imports.

The issue of July 2, 1853, indicates that it was then being published by Sheldon & Company of 55 Clark Street, which name appears to have been the style adopted by Reuben Sheldon, then cashier of the State Bank at the same address. In the 1855-1856 Chicago directory, Reuben Sheldon is listed as an Exchange Broker. Just how long this publication appeared under that title is obscure. Sometime prior to October, 1859, however, the title of Sheldon's reporter was changed to *The Chicago Bank Note List* with F. Granger Adams as the publisher.[39] Adams, as previously stated, was a son-in-law of John Thompson of New York.

In 1861, Adams published a "Descriptive List of Genuine Bank Notes" which was furnished gratis to subscribers of *The Chicago Bank Note List.* In this descriptive list is found the following detailed description of the periodical that sponsored its publication:

The "Chicago Bank Note List" is a western paper—gives a western value to western funds—and its editor confidently asserts is equal in every point to any paper of the kind, East or West. Business men of the West are invited to compare it with any Bank Note Detector published —if they find it what it claims to be, to subscribe.

[39] *Lee's Bank Note Register and Counterfeit Detecter* (Adv.), Buffalo: October 22, 1859.

In the Chicago Bank Note List will at all times be found a full list of all the solvent banks in the United States and Canadas—the rates at which the notes will be taken in Chicago—a full and complete Price Current, corrected with great care for each number, with a general summary of all such matters as bear on the money and stock market of the West.

Adams appears to have continued as publisher at least until July 15, 1862, according to the issue of that date. This issue, the only intervening one found subsequent to one in 1853, does not show a volume or issue number. The issue of this reporter for October 15, 1863, carries on the cover page the statement "Established 1853," which appears to substantiate the statement that *The Chicago Bank Note List* was a continuation of Sheldon's reporter. Notice was given that the information contained therein was corrected by the Traders' Bank and that communications should be addressed to S. K. Reed at 24 Clark Street. It would appear that F. Granger Adams, then interested in the Traders' Bank, had after several years turned over the publication of *The Chicago Bank Note List* to Silas K. Reed, a printer of Chicago.

The issue of June 1, 1863, shows on its cover page the volume and serial number, Vol. XI, No. 11. On the basis of a change of volume number annually, this reference appears to further substantiate that *The Chicago Bank Note List* was a continuation of Sheldon's reporter. The issue of November 16, 1863, is described as Vol. XI, No. 22, with S. K. Reed as publisher. The Chicago directories for 1863-1864 and 1864-1865 list *The Chicago Bank Note List* with S. K. Reed as publisher. It no doubt discontinued publication in 1865, and no periodicals of this type are found listed in *Halpin's Chicago Directory* for 1866.

Under the respective sponsorships of Reuben Sheldon, F. Granger Adams and Silas K. Reed, this reporter appears to have been published continuously for about twelve years from 1853 to 1865.

POOLE

According to *D. B. Cooke & Co.'s Chicago Directory* for 1857-1858, Isaac A. Poole, a dealer in books and maps, was the publisher of *The North-Western Bank Note and Counterfeit Detector,* a semi-monthly. His address was 17 S. Clark Street and quotations were by Church & Co., of 48 S. La Salle Street.

WILLARD AND YOUNG

Edward K. Willard and Caryl Young, bankers of 2 S. Clark Street, according to *Cooke's Directory* for 1859-1860, were publishers of a bank note reporter. While they are listed in the 1857-1858 and 1861-1862 directories as bankers, there is no indication that they published a bank note reporter during those periods.

TINKHAM

The Chicago directory for 1861-1862 lists Edward I. Tinkham, of the banking firm of E. I. Tinkham & Co., as the publisher of a bank note reporter. His firm in 1862-1863 was reported to have been "In liquidation," at which time he is listed as being cashier of the Traders' Bank.

PHILLIPS

Sometime in 1859 or 1860, Bezaleel W. Phillips, a banker of 8 S. Clark Street, sponsored the publication, monthly and semi-monthly, of *Phillips' North Western Money Reporter and Insurance Journal.* According to *Cooke's Directory* for 1860-1861, Phillips' name appears to have been dropped from the title, and George W. Kendrick, a banker, formerly of Port Byron, New York, is listed as publisher. Alexander Mayer of 8 Clark Street is named as the editor.

The Chicago directories for 1861-1862 and 1862-1863 show B. W. Phillips as the publisher of the *North Western Money Reporter,* at which time it was issued weekly, semi-weekly and monthly. It is not listed in the directory for 1863-1864.

McElroy

About 1862 or 1863, Solon McElroy, a banker, who some two or three years earlier had been general agent for the British Commercial Life Insurance Company, began the publication semimonthly and monthly of *McElroy's Bank Note Reporter*.

The Chicago directory for 1864-1865 indicates that he continued its publication at least until that time. The directory for 1865-1866 shows him only as secretary of the Chicago Stock Exchange.

Cincinnati

Cincinnati, laid out in 1789, was one of the first settlements in the Northwest Territory. The opening of steam navigation on the Ohio River in 1816, followed in 1830 by the completion of the Miami Canal, connecting Lake Erie with the Ohio River, brought rapid development of river and canal traffic, making this city an important river port.

Goodman

It was not until about July, 1840, that the *Western Counterfeit Detector and Bank Note Table*, a monthly in pamphlet form, made its appearance in Cincinnati. It was published by Charles Goodman under the supervision of H. H. Goodman & Co., exchange brokers. Sometime prior to July, 1845, the title was changed to *Western Counterfeit Detector, Bank Note Table, and Cincinnati Wholesale Prices Current*. At that time it was published at the office of T. S. Goodman & Co., exchange brokers. Under the same sponsorship the issue of May, 1847, shows another change of title to Goodman's *Western Counterfeit Detector, Bank Note Table, Cincinnati Wholesale Prices Current*.

In 1853, W. McCammon, Jr., appears as the publisher and in 1855, Wm. H. Ongley is found acting in the same capacity. Goodman's detector is not listed in *Williams' Cincinnati Directory* for 1856, and we can probably assume that its publication was discontinued sometime in 1855. In 1858, T. S. Goodman was appointed cashier of the Chillicothe branch of the State Bank of Ohio.[40]

T. W. LORD—THOS. R. LORD & CO.—JOHNSON BROS. & CO.—BEPLER & CO.

About 1842, T. W. Lord appears to have sponsored the publication of a bank note reporter in Zanesville, Ohio. Confirmation of this statement is found in the January, 1848, issue (No. LXVII, Vol. VI) of the *Zanesville Counterfeit Detector, and Bank Note Reporter* with T. W. Lord as its editor and proprietor. This issue was in pamphlet form and while the date line carries no place of publication, two advertisements of Zanesville merchants appear on the first page.

Under date of June, 1849, issue No. LXXXIV (Vol. VII) of *Cincinnati Counterfeit Detector and Bank Note Reporter* was published under the sponsorship of T. W. Lord as editor and proprietor. This publication was also in pamphlet form, of good format and contained, in addition to the usual information found in such publications, sixteen pages of facsimiles of the various gold and silver coins most generally found in circulation. Contained therein is an announcement that it was "Printed on the Steam Press of Wright, Fisher & Co., Gazette Office, 112 Main Street, Cincinnati." The typography and format of the two aforementioned reporters clearly indicate that they were printed from the same style of type and probably in the same office. The claimed circulation of this reporter at that time was 5,000 and the information therein was corrected by M. A. Bradley & Co., owners of the Phoenix Bank, who offered to receive all notes as quoted. The volume and issue number seem to indicate quite clearly that this reporter was a successor to the *Zanesville Counterfeit Detector and Bank Note Reporter*, and the following account will tend to confirm that statement.

Under date of March, 1850, issue No. 93 (Vol. VIII) of *Bradley &*

---

[40] *The Bankers' Magazine*, etc., New York: June, 1858, p. 974.

Co's Cincinnati Counterfeit Detector and Bank Note Reporter was published with T. W. Lord as editor and proprietor. It claimed a circulation at that time of 8,000. In this number, the editor in commenting upon the success of this publication made this interesting statement: "Twenty months only have elapsed since the first number was published in this city, ..." Comparison of the issue and volume numbers of this reporter with those of the Zanesville reporter, previously mentioned, leaves little doubt that Lord was located in Zanesville prior to moving to Cincinnati.

This publication continued for several years. T. W. Lord & Co., exchange brokers, are listed as the publishers of a bank note reporter in the Cincinnati directories from 1853 to 1856, after which the name of T. R. Lord appears irregularly for several years. In 1854, it was known as *Lord's Detector and Bank Note Reporter*. The issue of September 15, 1857 (monthly Vol. 16–No. 183) (semi-monthly Vol. 5–No. 107), is entitled *Lord's Detector and Bank Note Vignette Describer* and, while published by Thos. R. Lord & Co., of Cincinnati, the following places are indicated on the date line, "Cincinnati, New-York & St. Louis." An inside page carries this statement: "Established in 1842." This publication, while containing discount rates and descriptions of counterfeits, found in typical bank note reporters, also included descriptions of genuine vignettes which were a feature of the "descriptive lists." (*See* pp. 142-145.) Another feature is found in its method of listings. A small cut of a wildcat is shown opposite the statement "indicates a 'Wild-Cat' concern" (Plate XVIII). This same cut appears after the names of several organizations in the reporter to indicate that they are wildcat banks. Lord's detector is listed in all directories from 1859 to 1867. In 1857, Johnson Bros. & Co. took over its publication, and in the 1860's it was published by Bepler & Co.

In 1861 and for some years prior thereto, Bepler & Co. were the publishers of *Bepler's Bank Notes-Lists*, printed in German. This was at one time a forty page pamphlet, and the April 1, 1861, issue carries in the date line "Cincinnati, St. Louis and Chicago." A publication known as *Lord's Detector* was published in St. Louis, and may have had some connection with this series of publications.

John S. Dye

As heretofore stated, John S. Dye of New York appears to have sponsored the publication of *Dye's Counterfeit Detector and Universal Bank Note Gazetteer* in Cincinnati about 1850. Dye published in Cincinnati in 1852 *Dye's Bank Mirror and Illustrated Counterfeit Detector*. No information was obtained as to the period of existence of these publications.

General Counterfeit Detector

In 1850, Richard Smith is found as the publisher of *General Counterfeit Detector*, a monthly.[41] No further information was obtained and no copies of this reporter were found.

Langdon, Hawes & Co.

From about 1856 to 1860, Langdon, Hawes & Co. were publishers of *Cincinnati Safety Fund Bank Note Reporter*. Nothing was found that connected this publication with any others in Cincinnati, nor was any further information discovered.

White's Reporter and Counterfeit Detector

About 1859-1861, The Union Bank Reporter Publishing Company located at Walnut and Fifth Streets, in Cincinnati, sponsored the publication of *White's Reporter and Counterfeit Detector*, a monthly. No further information was found with respect to this reporter.

Union Counterfeit Detector

The Cincinnati directory for 1862 and 1863 lists *Union Counterfeit Detector*, a monthly, as being published at that time. This pub-

[41] Williams' *Cincinnati Almanac, Business Guide and General Advertiser*, 1850.

lication may have been the successor to the aforementioned reporter.

DETROIT

DAVID PRESTON & CO.

About 1855, David Preston & Co., exchange brokers and bankers of Detroit, Michigan, began the publication of *Preston's Bank Note Reporter*. It continued for at least ten years and the only copy found (Vol. 8, No. 5) is dated March 1, 1864, at which time it was known as *Preston's Detroit and Chicago Bank Note Reporter*. It is about quarto in size and was published semi-monthly at that time. This reporter probably circulated in Chicago as well as Detroit, as David Preston was also a member of the firm of Preston, Willard & Kean, Bankers, at No. 1 Clark Street, Chicago.

BROWN

Under date of January 1, 1859, J. H. Kaple & Co., bankers of Detroit, issued the first number of *Brown's Bank Note Reporter* with J. Brown as editor. It was a weekly, about quarto in size. It was probably short lived, as were many others, as its names does not appear in the Detroit directories after 1859. A complete weekly file from January 1, 1859, to July 1, 1859, inclusive (Nos. 1-25) was found. This probably constitutes the full period of existence of this reporter.

MONTGOMERY

In 1855, Samuel Swan of Montgomery, Alabama, published *Swan's Bank Note List and Detector*. It was said at that time to have been issued monthly at two dollars per annum. A notice of this publication indicated that "There is a variety of useful information in the work, in addition to a copious list of new and old counterfeits." [42]

Swan was an energetic and ambitious business man in Mont-

[42] *The Bankers' Magazine*, etc., New York: December, 1855, p. 492.

gomery and about 1851 he published a lithograph by Sarony entitled "The Burning of the Capital December 14, 1849." He also printed and sold lottery tickets, and conducted several lotteries in behalf of projects in the State of Alabama.

In 1856, this reporter was said to have been published semi-monthly, when it consisted of "some 40 quarto pages devoted to a list of all the banks in the United States, description of counterfeit bills, and a variety of other information of great value to merchants and bankers." [43] No copies of this reporter were discovered, nor was its period of existence ascertained.

Montreal

A bank note reporter was published in Montreal, Canada, in 1861, according to Kenny's *The American Newspaper Directory and Record of the Press.* No further information was found with respect to this reporter.

Philadelphia

Robert T. Bicknell — Imlay & Bicknell

In 1830, when there were approximately 330 banks operating in this country, Robert T. Bicknell, a lottery broker in Philadelphia, began the publication of a bank note reporter and counterfeit detector. He was the pioneer in this field in Philadelphia and was preceded only by Mahlon Day and S. J. Sylvester in New York. The first number, in folio form, dated July 31, 1830, appeared as *Bicknell's Counterfeit Detector, and Pennsylvania Reporter of Bank Notes, Broken Banks, Stocks, etc.* In this number the following reprint of his original prospectus is found:

It is handsomely printed on a super-royal sheet, with good type, contains a vast quantity of reading matter, as well as a list of prices current, a bank note list, and all such information as is calculated to prove serviceable to the man of business, country merchant and storekeeper.

[43] *The Merchants' Magazine*, etc., New York: August, 1858, Vol. 35, p. 217.

It will be issued every two weeks, is published on Saturday, embraces the latest foreign and other intelligence up to that period, and will be sent by mails which leave the city on the day of publication. The terms of the *Counterfeit Detector* will be Two Dollars per annum, payable in advance.

For about six months this reporter was published semi-monthly and then became a weekly. Several title changes took place during its existence. In June, 1831, the title was changed to *Bicknell's Reporter, Counterfeit Detector, and Prices Current,* and in February, 1835, to *Bicknell's Reporter, Counterfeit Detector, and Philadelphia Prices Current.* The issue of July 19, 1836, appeared as *Bicknell's Counterfeit Detector, and Pennsylvania Reporter of Bank Notes,* and the title again changed the following week to *Bicknell's Reporter, Counterfeit Detector, and General Prices Current* under which it continued until June 30, 1857, when it ceased publication in large folio form.

In October, 1832, Bicknell announced that having had frequent applications made to him for his List of Counterfeits and Altered Notes, and Bank Note List, in pamphlet form, he had concluded for the convenience of his numerous friends and the public to issue an edition in that form. The pamphlet edition, a monthly, first appeared on October 1, 1832, as *Bicknell's Counterfeit Detector and Bank Note List.* It contained items regarding finance, banks and banking, the usual bank note list, list of counterfeit and altered notes, a few advertisements and a table headed "Bank Note Exchange," arranged by States with the rates of discount on State bank notes at Philadelphia, Pittsburgh, Baltimore, New York and Boston. The weekly newspaper edition was referred to as the "Reporter" and the monthly pamphlet edition as the "Detector." The first named did not carry at all times a description of counterfeit and altered notes. The following announcement in Bicknell's own words with respect to his pamphlet edition may be of interest:

On the first of October last [1832], the subscriber, publisher of the "Reporter, Counterfeit Detector and Prices Current," issued his Bank Note List, and List of Counterfeits and Altered Notes, in pamphlet form, thinking that in that form it would be more convenient for the use of those who refer to his lists as a guide as to the genuineness of a note or otherwise. The success of this publication has been beyond his most sanguine expectations. Up to this time [May 1833] he has printed the seventh edition, and has sold about Twenty-five Thousand copies. This unexpected success, together with the urgent solicitations of many friends and patrons, has induced him to make such arrangements as will enable him to issue "The Counterfeit Detector and Bank Note List," hereafter, in pamphlet form, eight times a year, or every six weeks, in a new and improved manner, and carefully corrected. The first regular number of this series was commenced on Friday, the first of March. Each number will contain a carefully corrected Bank Note List, giving the names and places of location of all the banks in the United States, together with the rates of discounts on the notes of each. Prices of Gold and Silver. Also a correct description of Counterfeit and Altered notes, which are now, or have been in circulation, on each of the various Banking Institutions.

The pamphlet will be published on a royal sheet, and will contain twenty-four pages. Terms only $1 per annum, payable in all cases in advance.[44]

Bicknell, in an attempt to obtain some free advertising, made this statement following the above announcement: "The publisher of any newspaper in the United States who will give the above advertisement one or two insertions, and notice the 'Detector' editorially, will receive the Pamphlet regularly for two years." (*See* p. 114 for reference to a Boston Edition.)

The pamphlet form changed later to a monthly edition until sometime prior to March 1, 1845, when it was issued semi-monthly. After the pamphlet edition began, the table of counterfeit and altered notes did not appear in every edition of the weekly publica-

---

[44] *Bicknell's Counterfeit Detector and Bank Note List*, Philadelphia, Vol. I, No. 2, (May, 1833).

tion. In 1850, the weekly publication (in newspaper form) is accredited with a circulation of 4,000 and the semi-monthly publication (in pamphlet form) with a circulation of 5,000.

The weekly reporter of May 14, 1839, was published with all columns bordered with a heavy black stripe and the leading editorial announced the death of Robert Thaxter Bicknell on May 7, 1839— thirty-three years old. Bicknell in his will bequeathed his establishment to Matthew T. Miller, a near relative, who for many years had been associated with the concern as cashier. Miller announced that the Reporter would be published as heretofore. Matthew T. Miller continued the publication of the weekly reporter and the semi-monthly detector until June 30, 1857, when he announced that his time "being fully occupied in other and more profitable business, he has determined to relinquish the publication of the weekly Reporter." He also announced that the "Detector (pamphlet edition) will continue to be issued on the first and sixteenth of each month, and for the future will be published by Mr. Charles P. Bicknell," the only surviving son of the original proprietor.

Only a few issues of this publication were found subsequent to 1857, and it has not been possible to record accurately its history after that date. The Philadelphia city directory for 1859, however, lists "Imlay's & Bicknell's Bank Note Reporter." It appears that Mr. Charles G. Imlay, president of the Washington Insurance Company and cashier of the State Saving Fund, joined Mr. Charles P. Bicknell as a partner in the continuance of this venture. In 1862, it was published by Charles C. Rhodes for the proprietors, and the bank note list was corrected by Work, McCouch & Co. It is found listed under the foregoing title in the Philadelphia city directories from 1859 to 1866 inclusive. While no definite information was found as to when it ceased publication, it probably occurred in 1866, when the imposition of a ten per cent tax on State bank notes made the need of such publications unnecessary. The Bicknell publications covered a span of at least thirty-six years, being the longest period covered by any such publication during the State bank note era.

While, as previously stated, relatively few copies of these publications survive today, this is not the case with respect to Bicknell's weekly reporter in newspaper form. With the exception of a few scattered numbers in the first two years of its existence, a complete file of this reporter from 1830 to 1857 may be found in the Mercantile Library of Philadelphia.[45] They no doubt contain considerable source material on banks and banking during that interesting period.

MONTGOMERY'S

In 1841, the statement was made, "No less than three counterfeit detectors were published in this city [Philadelphia]—Bicknell's, Montgomery's and Van Court's." [46] One Robert Montgomery was an exchange broker in 1840, and in A. M'Elroy's *Philadelphia City Directory* for 1842 he is listed as the publisher of *U. S. Reporter and Counterfeit Detector*. No copies or any other reference to this reporter were found.

PETERSON'S

In 1858, a reporter under the sponsorship of T. B. Peterson & Brothers, 306 Chestnut Street, Philadelphia, made its appearance. Its inception was announced in the following newspaper editorial under a caption entitled "Varieties":

A New Counterfeit Detector—There are a great many counterfeit detectors published, mostly emanating from the city of New York. T. B. Peterson announces that he intends to publish one for Philadelphia, which will be as full of its information respecting counterfeits, broken banks and rates of discount on bank notes, as it is possible to make it. It will be placed under careful supervision. Drexel & Co., of this city, will make the corrections. Not being intended to subserve the purpose

---

[45] *See* appendix for source of copies of the pamphlet edition.
[46] William M. Gouge, *The Journal of Banking*, Philadelphia: July 21, 1841, Vol. I, No. 2.

of any particular banking house, as the New York detectors mostly are, it will be a useful and reliable publication for the business community. Its title will be Peterson's Philadelphia Counterfeit Detector and Bank Note List, and it will appear about the beginning of the new year.[47]

Two days later the following advertisement appeared under a caption entitled "New Publications":

COUNTERFEIT DETECTOR—NEW AND RELIABLE ONE

Peterson's Philadelphia Counterfeit Detector and Bank Note List.

To be published monthly, in a large page, 48 pages in each number on the first of each month, the first number being dated January 1st, 1858, and to be ready on Wednesday, December 23rd.

Drexel & Co., Bankers to Correct it.

The corrections in the Bank Note List as relates to the discount on Notes; Lists of new Counterfeits, etc. will be made by the well known Banking House of Drexel & Co., 34 South Third Street. And they will purchase all Bank Bills at the quotations made therein. This Detector will be found to be

RELIABLE AND TRUE

The publisher has for a long time seen the necessity and want of an entirely CORRECT, INDEPENDENT AND RELIABLE COUNTERFEIT DETECTOR AND BANK NOTE LIST, to be entirely uncontrolled by anyone to suit their own ends and purposes, and is confident that from the means and sources of information which the Editors of this Detector will have at their command, that it will be found to be the most RELIABLE Detector ever published in this country....[48]

The Peterson Magazine, devoted to art, fashions and light literature, was published at the same address and its publisher, C. J. Peterson, in the issue of November, 1858 (p. 371), states "... that Peterson Magazine has no connection with T. B. Peterson & Broth-

---

[47] *The Public Ledger* (Philadelphia), December 5, 1857.
[48] *Ibid.*, December 7, 1857.

ers." This notice appears to raise some question as to the reputation and standing of this reporter and may have been a sequence of the following account that appeared in *The Bank Note Register and Counterfeit Detecter,* Buffalo, for June 2, 1859, as reprinted from *The Bank Mirror* (no location nor date):

Imlay & Bicknell's Reporter of Philadelphia, has the following palpable hit at a contemporary who publishes a *Detecter* as an adjunct to the advertisements of "yellow-kivered literature," and who has discovered more *"new"* (?) counterfeits the last year than would fill his book twice over—In every issue heralding forth, with startling capitals, a prodigious number, the greatest part of which are much older than the work itself, and *new* to nobody but its novel-writing editor. Imlay says:

A Novel Detecter.—It is said that a Detecter in this city [Philadelphia] announces more new novels than new counterfeits. Out of the 66 announced as new in its April issue, we observe some 40 almost grey with age.

Some few months later another announcement, referring to the February, 1860, number of this reporter, is couched in the following more favorable tone:

One great feature of Peterson's Detector is a page of information on finance, locally and generally, written expressly for this work by one of the least visionary writers in this country.[49]

McElroy's Philadelphia City Directory lists Peterson's detector annually from 1860 to 1867. Its name is not found in the 1867-1868 directory.

Storm & Morgan

Storm & Morgan, Exchange Brokers, located at 51 South 3rd Street, Philadelphia, in 1842, were the publishers about that time of *Bank Note Rates of Exchange and Counterfeit Detector.* This was another short-lived reporter as evidenced by the following an-

---

[49] *The Daily Guardian* (Paterson, New Jersey), February 13, 1860.

nouncement in *Van Court's Counterfeit Detector and Bank Note List* for June, 1843:

*Bank Note Rates of Exchange
and
Counterfeit Detector
1843*

The list of subscribers of the above named publication has been transferred to J. Van Court, Esq. Our subscribers will accordingly be hereafter served with "Van Court's Counterfeit Detector."

(Signed) STORM & MORGAN

Phila. May 27, 1843

No further information was obtained with respect to this detector and no copies were found.

VAN COURT'S

From 1830 until just prior to his death in May, 1839, Robert T. Bicknell had the field to himself in Philadelphia in so far as bank note reporters were concerned. Under date of February 14, 1839, a new monthly reporter appeared under the title *Philadelphia Reporter, Counterfeit Detector, Philadelphia Prices Current, and General Advertiser.* The publisher was John Libby, the printer, J. Van Court, and the subscription rate one dollar per annum.

A detailed statement of the contents and the aims of the publisher as it appeared in the first issue follows:

The Philadelphia Reporter, the first number of which is now presented to the public, has been undertaken from a conviction that a work of the kind—so cheap as to place it in the reach of every person—was needed. The country is literally flooded with spurious paper, that is, counterfeit notes—and the unsuspecting and those who are less able to sustain loss, are the persons who generally suffer most. The amount lost annually by the farmer, the mechanic, and persons in a small way of business, is enormous—the merchants and all through whose hands large amounts of paper money pass, come in for a share—while innkeepers and traders are peculiarly liable to imposition. The best way to guard against impositions in the receipt of bank notes, is correct information, so as to enable a person to decide with accuracy between the genuine and the counterfeit. So far as this very desirable end may be accomplished, through the agency of the press, it will be attempted; and for this purpose we shall publish from time to time, a full, complete and correct description of all known counterfeit notes in circulation, as in the present number: and also keep the public advised of all new counterfeits, alterations and frauds. The reader will also find a description of Frauds—a list of Closed and Broken Banks. The value in the city of Philadelphia, of the notes of the different Banks throughout the Union—the Prices of Stocks, etc.—the whole revised and corrected for each publication by a gentleman who has for years past been connected with the money and stock markets, and whose opportunities of obtaining correct and early information on all subjects connected with his profession, is equal to that of any other.

The Prices Current, will receive particular attention. The prices of the principal articles will be corrected by gentlemen extensively engaged in mercantile pursuits. Every effort will be made to render the table as correct as the fluctuating state of trade will render possible.

The remainder of the paper will be occupied by the News of the day—Miscellaneous reading—Statistical information—intelligence respecting the money market, agriculture, commerce, trade, the mechanic arts, &c. We have thus briefly given an outline of the paper. We make no promises further than that we bring what industry and talent we possess to the work. The present number we submit as a sample of its general execution—and we hope so to conduct it as to render it an acceptable visitor in the counting house of the merchant—the store of the trader—the shop of the mechanic—the dwelling of the farmer—in all places of business, and among all classes who may be benefitted by it.

Messrs. Prouty, Libby and Prouty appeared as the publishers of the third number. The October, 1839 (No. 9), issue shows a change of title to *Philadelphia Reporter, Counterfeit Detector and Prices Current* at which time the publishers stated that "at the suggestion of our many friends we have changed the form from quarto to octavo." In December of the first year, the publishers transferred their interests to John Van Court, who preferred to be known as "J. Van Court." He was a printer in Philadelphia for about thirty-five years.

In September, 1840, the title of this reporter was changed to *Philadelphia Counterfeit Detector and Bank Note List.* The final change in title took place with the issue of December, 1841, when it took the name of its publisher and printer and was thereafter known as *Van Court's Counterfeit Detector and Bank Note List.*

In the issue of March 7, 1842, the following notice is found:

At the suggestion of a number of our friends and subscribers, we have determined to issue a small sheet, (large enough, however, to answer our purpose) every week, except the week in which our regular monthly is issued. 2 pp. In order to keep the public apprised of the various changes which are taking place almost daily in the value of our paper money.

Price 6¼ cts., every Friday morning.

In issue No. 3 of this sheet, notice was given that the price had been reduced to three cents, and on August 19, 1842, Van Court announced that in the present stagnation of business this publication was not needed every week and that in the future it would be issued about the middle of the month. This "small sheet" was continued at least until June 15, 1844 (No. 32).

Van Court was jealous of the good reputation he had built up over a number of years and in 1857, the day after a large advertisement announcing the publication of a new reporter appeared in a local newspaper, he caused the following notice (in part), with respect to his reporter, to be published:

This Detector (established 1839) is as correct, reliable, well arranged, and complete, as any work of the kind can be made. This assertion is made understandingly, after an experience of nearly twenty years. And when any men or set of men, attempt to make the public believe, through flashy advertisements and paid editorials, that they are about to issue a better and more reliable work of the kind than was ever before published, that same public will begin to suspect, as well it may, that there is in the whole thing a strong *squinting* of HUMBUG.

Van Court's Counterfeit Detector is fully equal (we do not say superior) to any other work of the kind, especially in the arrangement, the States being placed in alphabetical order, and having a marginal alphabetical Index, thus making it very convenient for reference. The most untiring efforts are made to furnish a correct and competent Detector, and Note List, with the rates of discount, descriptions of counterfeits, prices of stocks, list of broken banks, etc.[50]

In many instances it has not been possible to establish the exact date when the publication of a particular reporter was discontinued. That is not the case with Van Court's. The following footnote, in ink, is found at the bottom of the first page of the issue of December, 1858 (Vol. XX, No. 12, Whole No. 239):

> The last number issued by J. V. C. Sold to Imlay
> & Bicknell who united it with their Reporter.
> (Signed) J. V. C.

The foregoing statement, apparently in the handwriting of the publisher, brought to a close the twenty year span of this reporter, which appears to have enjoyed a good reputation during its entire existence.

Pittsburgh

Pittsburgh in western Pennsylvania, where the Monongahela River and the Allegheny River meet to continue on as the Ohio River, was an important river point in the early years of the nineteenth century. The first bank note reporter, according to the following advertisement, came into existence there in 1838:

E. Sibbet & Co., Exchange Brokers, Pittsburgh, propose to issue a monthly publication under the title,—

[50] *The Public Ledger* (Philadelphia), December 8, 1857.

*Sibbet's Western Review Counterfeit
List and Monthly Report of the Currency and Markets*

The present unsettled state of the currency, and the great and increasing importance of the cities and towns of the west, both combine to render the proposed publication one of almost indispensable necessity.

The work will be printed on a small and elegant type.—Each number will contain twenty-four super-royal octavo pages.

The first number will be issued on the first of June, [1838], from which time it will continue to issue regularly on the first of every month.[51]

The subscription rate at that time was $1.50 per annum. Linton Rogers was general agent for Pittsburgh and vicinity. The publishers, E. Sibbet & Co., in 1836, advertised: "Drafts, Notes, and Bills, on any of the Banking Institutions of Pennsylvania, Ohio, Kentucky, Illinois, Indiana, &c., collected on the most reasonable terms. Western Bank Paper purchased and remitted for in eastern funds."[52]

In March, 1849, this reporter was known as *Sibbet's Western Review and Counterfeit Detector* (Vol. XII, March 1, 1849, No. 141), and was reported to have had a circulation of 3,000 in 1850. A change of name occurred in 1853, or prior thereto, as evidenced by the following advertisement:

Sibbet's Bank Note Review and Counterfeit Detector

It is the oldest Detector in the country with but one exception; being established in 1838, by Mr. Sibbet, then one of the principal bankers and exchange brokers of this city. It is now under the correcting supervision of S. Jones & Co., (formerly Sibbet & Jones,) one of the oldest and most firmly established firms in the west.

KENNEDY & BROTHER
Publishers and Proprietors.[53]

[51] *Sylvester's Reporter*, etc., May 21, 1838.
[52] *Harris' Pittsburgh Business Directory*, 1837.
[53] *Kennedy's Fac Simile Counterfeit Bank Note Detector & Coin Book*, 1853.

The statement that this publication "is the oldest Detector in the country with but one exception" is not borne out by the facts set forth herein. It was preceded by several years by Day's and Sylvester's in New York, Bicknell's in Philadelphia, and Thomas' in St. Louis. It was later succeeded by *Kennedy's Bank Note Review and Fac Simile Counterfeit Detector* which continued at least until 1856. The publishers of the last named periodical in January, 1854, issued an auxiliary to their counterfeit detector entitled *Western Price Current and Weekly Bank Note Review.*

The National Bank Reporter

According to a newspaper advertisement in 1865, Messrs. Feld and Lare, with offices in the Dispatch Building, Pittsburgh, Pennsylvania, were publishers of *The National Bank Reporter*. The April, 1865, issue was said to contain the latest information upon financial matters, counterfeit notes, etc. The subscription rate was two dollars per annum.[54]

There were two other reporters that appear to have been published in Pittsburgh around 1861, listed merely as *Bank Note Reporter* and *Bank Note Mirror*. The first named was said to be a weekly publication and the last named a semi-monthly and monthly publication.[55] The *Bank Note Mirror* may have been a local edition of one of John S. Dye's publications.

St. Louis

On February 14, 1764, a party of workmen landed at a point on the Mississippi River selected by Laclede for a trading post and settled on what is now the present site of St. Louis. It became an important center for traders who carried on an extensive traffic with the Indians on the Mississippi and Missouri Rivers. When Missouri was admitted to the Union in 1821, St. Louis had a population of

---

[54] *The Pittsburgh Dispatch*, April 15, 1865.
[55] **Daniel J. Kenny**, *The American Newspaper Directory and Record of the Press*, New York: 1861.

only 5,600, and it was some ten years later that the first bank note reporter was published there.

THOMAS

On January 20, 1832, the Hon. Thomas H. Benton, United States Senator from Missouri, delivered a speech in the Senate of the United States which related to a resolution on the state of the currency. In this speech he referred to *Thomas' Counterfeit Note Detector* of St. Louis and quotes the following from the issue of that detector dated December 19, 1831: "The present number of the Detector contains the full list of all the different descriptions of counterfeit and altered notes that have been presented at my counter [the publisher's] since the publication of the first number on the 28th of April [1831]. You will find it has 159." Thomas conducted a brokerage office in St. Louis. Senator Benton also quoted this statement which appeared in the *Missouri Monitor* of January 1, 1832:

The numerous counterfeits on the various Branches of the Bank of the United States has given rise to a new description of newspapers in St. Louis and many other places—necessary, and intended solely to guard the community against spurious Bank notes! The December number of Thomas' Counterfeit Note Detector exposes one hundred and fifty-nine varieties of counterfeit Bills.

This detector, the first to be published in St. Louis, appears to have been ante-dated by but three others: Day's and Sylvester's in New York City and Bicknell's in Philadelphia. No copies of this detector were found and its period of existence was not ascertained.

PRESBURY & COMPANY

Presbury and Company's Counterfeit Detector was published in St. Louis in 1849. This periodical is referred to in the *Minnesota Pioneer* of January 9, 1850.[56] It was probably sponsored by George

---
[56] Sydney A. Patchin, "Banking in Minnesota," *Minnesota History Bulletin*, Vol. II (August, 1917), p. 122.

G. Presbury & Company who are listed as bankers in *Green's St. Louis Directory* for 1851. They were located at that time at 103½ N. Main Street, St. Louis. No copies were found and no further information was obtained with respect to this reporter.

CLARK

In November, 1842, the banking firm of E. W. Clark & Brothers was established in St. Louis. This was the first branch to be added to the old stock and exchange brokerage house of Enoch W. Clark of Philadelphia, with which Jay Cooke, the noted financier of the Civil War, was long identified.[57]

This firm sponsored the publication of a counterfeit detector. While the date established was not definitely ascertained, it was, however, published as early as 1853, according to the following statement which appeared in *The Bankers Magazine and Statistical Register* for April, 1853, as quoted from an article in the *St. Louis Republican* (no date given) regarding Illinois bank notes: "On referring to Clark's Counterfeit Detector we find the following banks doing business in Illinois under the General Banking Law, ..." Then followed a list of several banks. The St. Louis directory for 1859 indicates that Robert L. Clarke was the publisher at that time. Just when this reporter ceased publication was not ascertained. It was found listed, however, in 1861, as being in existence at that time.[58]

ST. LOUIS BANK NOTE REPORTER

The St. Louis directory for 1860 lists Horatio Page as the editor of the *St. Louis Bank Note Reporter,* published on the first and fifteenth of each month. The reporter was also found listed as being in existence in 1861.[59]

Two other reporters were listed as having been published in St.

---

[57] Henrietta M. Larson, *Jay Cooke, Private Banker,* 1936, p. 54.
[58] Daniel J. Kenny, *op. cit.*
[59] *Ibid.*

Louis. *Bank Note Detector* was described as a monthly, with a circulation of 1,000.[60] The other, listed as *Lord's Detector,* was published at least from 1859 to 1861. In 1859, its publishers were Johnson, Phillips and Company and in 1860, "Lord's Detector Office" was located at 251 Broadway. This periodical may have had some connection with the Lord publications that appeared in Cincinnati for many years.

ZANESVILLE

Zanesville Counterfeit Detector and Bank Note Reporter was published here from about 1842 to 1848 when its publisher moved to Cincinnati. For further details see under T. W. Lord in Cincinnati.

[60] *Livingston's Law Register*, 1852.

VI

CONTEMPORARY RELATED PUBLICATIONS

IT was common practice for publishers of bank note reporters to offer, in many instances gratis, to subscribers of their reporters, certain other publications of interest to those whose business dealings made it necessary for them to handle the confusing circulating media of the State bank note era. This record would be quite incomplete without some reference to these publications which took the form of descriptive lists of genuine notes, bank note plate delineators, facsimile signatures of bank officers, and coin chart manuals. There follow the names and a description of such publications that came to light during the compilation of this work.

Sylvester's Bank Note and Exchange Manual

In January, 1833, S. J. Sylvester issued in New York City a publication entitled *Sylvester's Bank Note and Exchange Manual*. It consisted of thirty-two pages, about octavo in size. Its prospectus contained the following description of its contents:

> This pamphlet is offered to the public as a convenient manual for businessmen generally, and it will be found a safe guide on the subject of the value of Bank Notes, as well as a Detector of Counterfeit Bills and the Rates of Exchange. The subscriber is induced to compile the information in this form from the fact that such a publication is called for by many of his patrons in preference to a newspaper. From his experience for many years as an Exchange Broker, and as publisher of "Sylvester's Reporter," a weekly paper now honored with an extensive patronage, the public may rely on the present publication for its correctness, and he has full confidence that it will be favorably received.

They were sold at 12½¢ each and contained a list of solvent banks, insolvent banks and fraudulent institutions, together with a list of counterfeit and altered notes.

Bank Note Descriptive Lists

Thompson — New York

John Thompson of New York at various times made available "to all subscribers of his bank note reporter who paid one year in advance" no less than three different supplements. One of these, entitled *Bank Note Descriptive List,* was described as containing accurate descriptions of all the "Genuine Bank Notes issued by the Banks in the United States and Canada."

The earliest copy discovered is dated 1859 (not numbered), about quarto in size, and contains upwards of eighty pages. In 1861, the Fourteenth Edition appeared, and in 1866 the Twenty-eighth Edition was published. Thompson's *Descriptive List* was published as late as 1867, then described as the "Thirty-First Edition." One unique feature of the Twenty-third Edition, a pamphlet of ninety-six pages and dated 1864, is that a facsimile of the State seal that appeared on many State bank notes at that time, as well as the Original Series of national bank notes, is shown preceding the descriptive list of notes of each State. These publications also contained a list of "broken" and "retired" banks.

The descriptive data of individual bank notes was rather brief and can best be illustrated by a reprint of the description of genuine notes issued in 1861 by The Cataract City Bank of Paterson, New Jersey.

Cataract City Bank, Paterson

1s, hogs, fowls, &c., in round die, ONE on left–1, die–ONE across. ¶

2s, waterfall, men at work, houses, &c. TWO on right, die, on left–2, TWO across–2, TWO. ¶

3s, Indian family on a cliff overlooking a city, THREE above them, THREE below–3, die–THREE. ¶ ☞

5s, signing Declaration of Independence, pale red 5 each side–5, arms–5, female portrait. ¶

10s, Penn's treaty with the Indians–10, Liberty surrounded by stars –X, arms. ¶

Contemporary Related Publications 143

In an explanation of the key, the publisher stated that "in giving a description of a genuine bill, we divide the note into four parts: 1st, The vignette; 2d, The right end; 3d, The left end; and 4th, The engraving (if any) between the President and Cashier's Signatures, each part separated by a dash (—)...." He also stated that an index (☞) means that there are imitation counterfeits on that particular plate and a paragraph sign (¶) denotes that the particular note is printed in colors, which effectually guards against photographic counterfeits.

Adams — Chicago

In 1861, F. Granger Adams (son-in-law of John Thompson), then the publisher of *The Chicago Bank Note List,* furnished to his subscribers a descriptive list of genuine bank notes almost identical in form to that of Thompson's *Bank Note Descriptive List.*

White — Cincinnati

The Union Bank Reporter Publishing Company in 1859 were the publishers of *The Describer of Genuine Bank Notes,* a supplement to *White's Reporter and Counterfeit Detecter.* It was octavo in size and consisted of seventy-six pages, containing "accurate descriptions of all the notes issued by the banks of the United States and Canada." It was given free to all subscribers of the reporter.

The only copy of this publication found indicates that it is none other than Thompson's *Descriptive List of Genuine Bank Notes* for the same year. Thompson's cover page has been detached and a new cover affixed. On page three, at the only place where Thompson's name and the title of his work appear, a paster about two by six inches in size has been used to cover them. This paster bears an imprint reading, "The Describer of Genuine Bank Notes—Supplementary to White's Bank Reporter."

Brown — Detroit

In 1859, a bank note descriptive list was furnished supplementary to *Brown's Bank Note Reporter* of Detroit. It is a pamphlet of seventy-six pages, similar in form to that of *Thompson's Bank Note Descriptive List*, which was given free of charge to all subscribers to the reporter who paid one year's subscription in advance.

Preston — Detroit

Preston's Detroit and Chicago Bank Note Reporter for March 1, 1864, indicates that subscriptions to their publication included a "descriptive list."

Hodges — New York

In 1859, J. Tyler Hodges, a bank note reporter publisher in New York, made available *Hodges' Genuine Bank Notes of America*. This publication followed the same format as that of Thompson's list. Apparently they both first appeared in 1859. Just who was the originator of this style of publication is not known. While it appears that Thompson issued at least thirty-one editions of his descriptive list, only one edition of Hodges' list was found. It is about 11½ by 9 inches in size and consists of forty pages. On the title page is found the following brief description of its contents: "The only original and correct work ever published, except the BANK NOTE SAFEGUARD, giving plain, succinct, and RELIABLE DESCRIPTIONS of every genuine bank note of every denomination on every bank in the UNITED STATES & CANADA."

Monroe's — New York

A publication entitled *Monroe's Descriptive List of Genuine Bank Notes* was in existence during the State bank note era. It was said to contain 1,323 separate descriptions of notes.[1] It was probably sponsored by John Monroe, who, in 1857 and 1858, was associated with John Tyler Hodges, a publisher of a bank note reporter at that time, and also a publisher of a descriptive list.

[1] Horace White, *Money and Banking*, 5th ed.; New York: 1914, p. 329.

Clarke's Descriptive List—St. Louis

According to an advertisement in the St. Louis directory for 1859, Robert L. Clarke was the publisher of *Clarke's Descriptive List of Genuine Bank Notes.*

Clark's Monetype — St. Louis

During the State bank note era a publication was issued under the above title and under the sponsorship of E. W. Clark & Brothers. It was described as being a pamphlet consisting of seventy-six pages (date not mentioned), containing descriptions and many facsimiles of the currency listed, and said to have been the only guide to "wild-cat currency" published in St. Louis.[2]

Dye's Bank Note Plate Delineator

This book is described by its publisher as a spurious and altered bill detector, giving printed descriptions of the genuine notes of every denomination of all the banks doing business throughout the United States and British North America. The publisher, John S. Dye, as previously stated was an exchange broker, located at 172 Broadway, corner of Maiden Lane, New York City, where he also published *Dye's Bank Mirror.*

Dye stated in part in the 1855 "Complete" edition, which appears to have been the first: "After three years of incessant toil this work has at length been completed. Perhaps no book, in this or any other language, has been got up at such expense, and we can safely say that none can surpass it in value for Commercial purposes."[3]

Dye stressed the point that no detector ever was published that described the genuine note, the force of all publications being directed towards the spurious, altered, and counterfeit notes. He goes on to say: "The most numerous class are spurious, notes that bear no

[2] Henrietta M. Larson, *Jay Cooke, Private Banker*, 1936, p. 58.
[3] *The Bankers' Magazine and Statistical Register*, May, 1855, p. 907, refers to *Dye's Bank Note Plate Delineator* and states that, "A useful publication has just been issued."

resemblance to the genuine, these are killed at sight, as you have in your own hand the likeness or daguerreotype of the genuine, and the dress and design of the two notes may be as different as that of a lady and gentleman." Dye pointed out further that: "The Delineator detects all past, present, and future spurious or altered notes, and has accomplished more to protect the Commercial interests of this country than all the Reporters and Detectors that have ever been published, for all they can do at most is to cry thief after the goods have been stolen."

The 1855 edition consists of 288 pages and contains the names of approximately 1,200 banks then in operation throughout the United States and Canada. Each page, twelve by seven inches in size, contains three columns of nine rectangular blocks about 1¼ inches wide by 2¼ inches long wherein is given a brief description of notes issued by the respective banks. (*See* Plate XIX.) No other "Complete" editions were found. The publisher, however, in the same year issued another edition similar in format entitled "Parts I & II." This edition contained the names and descriptions of notes of 419 banks located in New York, Massachusetts, Pennsylvania, and Maryland. In this edition the following statement was found (p. 133): "The third number of the Delineator will be published in a short time." No other editions were found.

Hodges' Safe-Guard

The aforementioned bank note plate delineator published by John S. Dye in 1855 appears to have had a rather brief existence. Another publisher, however, felt that there was a need for such a publication, and, in 1857, J. Tyler Hodges, the publisher of a bank note reporter, undertook the publication of *Hodges' New Bank Note Safe-Guard*. The description of the notes and the style in which they are presented is identical with that of Dye's *Delineator*, while the prospectus or introduction is so similar to that of Dye's that one is lead to believe that the entire work of Hodges in 1857

Contemporary Related Publications 147

was pirated from Dye's work in 1855, with no credit given to the latter for the originality exhibited by him. It will be noted later that there can be no question that Hodges' publication was originally prepared from the identical plates used by Dye.

In 1855, Dye stated that, "After three years of incessant toil this work has at length been completed." Hodges in 1857 stated that, "After years of toil and great expense, this work has at length been completed, ..." In 1855, Dye stated:

> The DELINEATOR detects all past, present, and future spurious or altered notes, and has accomplished more to protect the Commercial interests of the country than all the Reporters and Detectors that have ever been published, for all they can do at most is to cry thief after the goods have been stolen.

Along these same lines, Hodges in 1857 stated:

> In a word, THE SAFEGUARD detects all past, present and future spurious and altered notes, and is of more value, protection and security to the commercial interests of the country, than all the Detectors, Bank Note Lists, and other works, which up to this time have been published. In fact the SAFE-GUARD is almost indispensable, for it goes ahead of, and anticipates the counterfeiter, cutting off his success, while the Reporters and Bank Note Lists but follow after, and to use a homely, but forcible expression, "can only lock the stable after the horse is stolen."

Hodges also comments on the great superiority of the SAFE-GUARD over all reporters and bank note detectors notwithstanding the fact that he was the publisher of such a periodical at the same time. The foregoing statements questioning the originality of Hodges' publication have some confirmation when identical typographical errors in both publications are pointed out. In Dye's *Delineator* for 1855 and Hodges' *Safe-Guard* for 1857, a comparison of the index of New York banks discloses in both publications the following identical errors in the spelling of place names; Glens Falls as Glen*n*s Falls, Ithaca as Ith*i*ca, Onondaga as Onondag*o,* and West

Winfield as West Win*d*field. We find also on page 238 of each publication, "Central Bank" as "Central Ba*k*k."

Hodges' *Safe-Guard* was published in several editions over a period of about ten years.[4] It appears to have been first issued in 1857 as *Hodges' New Bank Note Safe-Guard,* having been arranged and published at that time by J. Tyler Hodges. It consisted of 326 pages as compared to Dye's *Delineator* for 1855 consisting of 288 pages. Other editions found were the 3rd Quarterly Edition in 1858, the 4th Quarterly Edition in 1858, the First Quarterly Edition in 1859, and the 4th Quarterly Edition in 1860, which had then expanded to 380 pages. The 1861 edition was published by Daniel M. Hodges, a brother of J. Tyler Hodges. His name also appears on a revised edition in 1861 with the title changed to *Hodges' American Bank Note Safe-Guard.* The 1862 revised edition was also published under the same sponsorship. Late in 1862, the following announcement with respect to this publication was made: "Our last edition, *the tenth,* revised and corrected to November 1, 1862, is now ready."[5] From this statement it appears that there were two or three editions besides those referred to above. The 1863 revised edition was published by Edwin M. Hodges, a son of Daniel M. Hodges, as was the 1864 edition and the revised edition of 1865. The last named was probably the last edition of this interesting publication, as no numbers bearing a later date were found.

Gwynne & Day's Descriptive Register

Gwynne & Day, bankers, with offices at 12 Wall Street, New York, were, in 1859, the publishers of a book entitled *The Descriptive Register of Genuine Bank Notes.* They stated that this register was for the detection of spurious and altered bills and contained accurate, elaborate and plain descriptions of the notes issued by every bank in the United States and Canada. They acknowledged

---

[4] *See* appendix for the location of some of the existing editions.
[5] *Hodges' Journal of Finance & Bank Reporter,* December 1, 1862.

"their indebtedness to the several firms now comprising The American Bank Note Company for much valuable information." This book, about 11½ by 8 inches in size, consists of 143 pages and contains the names of more than 1,400 banks with a brief description, in narrative form, of the genuine notes issued by those banks. They announced that a supplement to the book, containing a description of all new notes and the bills of all banks organized after its publication, would be issued as often as deemed necessary and would be given gratis to the subscribers of *The Bank Note Register* which was published under their sponsorship.

This register appeared in several editions, the following dates having been noted: 1859, 1860, 1862, 1863, and 1866, the last named being described as "The Fourteenth Edition." The 1862 edition was issued from the office of *The Metropolitan Bank Note Reporter*, while the 1866 edition was put out by H. J. Messenger, who was at that time the publisher of *Metropolitan National Bank Note Reporter*.

Kennedy's Descriptive List

According to the copyright registration imprint, Messrs. Kennedy and Brother of Pittsburgh published in 1857 a paper-covered book about eleven by seven inches in size consisting of 166 pages which was entitled *Description of Genuine Bank Notes*. It was published at the Kennedy Review Office in Pittsburgh, which concern also published a counterfeit detector.

The format of this register is quite similar to that of Gwynne & Day. It includes a description in narrative form of the notes issued by the banks of that period. The index of this book contains a list of all the banks in straight alphabetical sequence by name, rather than in sequence by states. It devotes 128 pages to the description of bank notes and 38 pages to the reproduction of facsimiles of gold and silver coins of the world. While the registration imprint is dated 1857, the back cover page contains a monthly calendar for the year

1861. Notes are described therein of several banks that suspended prior to 1860.

Kennedy's Fac Simile Counterfeit Note Detector

Kennedy and Brother of Pittsburgh also put out a publication entitled *Kennedy's Fac Simile, Ein Supplement Zu ihrem Vereinigte Staaten Banknoten Kenner (A Supplement To Their Bank Note Guide)*. This publication, about quarto in size, the text of which is in German, contains a number of full size illustrations of notes in circulation at the time, together with a list of closed banks. While undated, there appears on the outside cover page a calendar for the year 1853.

This same firm also published *Kennedy's Fac Simile Counterfeit Note Detector*. One issue appeared the same year as the previously described publication. Another issue of this same publication is dated 1856 and contained merely 32 full sized illustrations of counterfeit notes. It was described as a supplement to their *Western Review*.

The Autographical Counterfeit Detector

Probably the most unique publication in the banking field, during the period under review or at any other time, was that entitled *The Autographical Counterfeit Detector*. It was sponsored by John Thompson and in his reporter for January 23, 1851, he said, "This work is the greatest Autographical curiosity in the world, embracing over 1,500 Facsimile Signatures of the different Bank Officers in the United States."

The earliest edition located, a pamphlet of sixty pages, is dated 1849 and described as a companion to *The Bank Note Reporter*, given free to all weekly and semi-monthly subscribers to the reporter. Single copies were sold at twenty-five cents each. The information contained therein was compiled and arranged by J. Thompson, Stock and Exchange Broker, and published by Wm. W. Lee at No. 12 Spruce Street, New York City. The Fourth Edition

(1851) was a pamphlet of sixty-six pages, while the Fifth Edition (1853) and probably the last, less than octavo in size, consisted of seventy-five pages. It was said to contain the facsimile signatures of the president and cashier of *nearly* every bank in the United States.

Page 44 of the Fifth Edition (Plate XVII) shows among others the signature of the cashier of the Mohawk Valley Bank of Mohawk, New York, who at that time was none other than Francis E. Spinner who later served as Treasurer of the United States from March, 1861, to June, 1875. His striking signature is found on most of the United States currency issued during that period.

While the facsimile signatures presented in this detector were of great value to those handling State bank notes who might question the genuineness of signatures appearing thereon, they were no doubt of inestimable value to the swindler and crook engaged in counterfeiting such notes. For that reason alone it is rather surprising that such a publication ever existed.

Taylor's Signature Examiner

In 1849, C. S. Sloane, a specie and exchange broker, 23 Wall Street, New York City, published *Taylor's Signature Examiner*, it being a supplement to *Taylor's U. S. Money Reporter, and Gold and Silver Examiner*. This pamphlet, about octavo in size, consists of sixty-four pages and is described as containing "facsimile engravings of the signatures of the Presidents and Cashiers of all the banks in the Union." The engravings from which the signatures were printed were executed on wood by J. W. Orr, 75 Nassau Street, New York.

The object of this publication was as an aid in detecting counterfeit notes. Its format and contents was quite similar to that of Thompson's *The Autographical Counterfeit Detector*.

The following detailed description of its contents is found on the inside cover page:

As an aid in detecting Counterfeit Bank Notes, the Publisher has thought no more effectual means could be adopted than to publish facsimile Engravings of the Signatures of the Presidents and Cashiers of all the Banks in the Union.

The accompanying engravings are exact imitations of the signatures they represent, the greatest care having been taken both in drawing and engraving. The publisher, however, wishes it to be understood that he does not guarantee that the engravings given will correspond in every single line and mark with genuine signatures with which they may be compared, inasmuch as the various signatures of any person will vary more or less, he can only guarantee the general character and expression of the signatures to be correct.

The Banks are arranged by States, in the same order as in the MONEY REPORTER, Subscribers to the "Money Reporter," are entitled to a copy of the SIGNATURE EXAMINER, free of extra charge; and will receive a fresh copy when ever any alterations are made. Monthly subscribers to the "Reporter" will be served one year for one dollar—three copies for two dollars.

CHARLES & LEONORI'S SIGNATURE EXAMINER

About 1850, Charles & Leonori began the publication of a bank note reporter, which, as previously related, appears to have been the successor of two other reporters, one of which was established by one Taylor for whom the above signature examiner was named.

This firm, in about 1850, issued a signature examiner, which was, except for the cover pages, prepared from the identical plates from which Taylor's examiner was printed. It is entitled *Charles & Leonori's (Late Taylor's) Signature Examiner*.

COIN CHART MANUALS

Another supplement to *Thompson's Bank Note and Commercial Reporter* was known as *The Coin Chart Manual*. It appeared as early as 1848. An advertisement in *The Autographical Counterfeit Detector* for 1849 describes *The Coin Chart Manual* as containing over eight hundred and fifty facsimiles of various gold and silver coins found in circulation. It was sent free to every regular yearly subscriber of the *Reporter*. Single copies were sold at 12½ cents each. The edition of 1853, about octavo in size, contains fifty-six pages, and was described as containing "1125 fac-similes of the various gold and silver coins found in circulation." This manual was published at least until 1877. The "thoroughly revised" edition (Vol. 45) of that year was described as "containing the facsimiles of all the gold and silver coins found in circulation throughout the world, with the intrinsic value of each."

A coin chart manual, somewhat similar in style to that of Thompson, was furnished as a supplement to several other reporters. In 1847, S. Taylor put out *Taylor's Gold and Silver Coin Examiner*, a pamphlet of sixteen pages; in 1853, Bicknell (Philadelphia) issued *The American Book of Coins* (48 pp.); about 1854, *Dye's Gold and Silver Coin Chart Manual* was published by John S. Dye in both New York and Cincinnati; around 1855, Hodges (New York) published *Hodges' Gold and Silver Coin Chart Manual*; about 1859, *Peterson's* (Philadelphia) *Complete Coin Book* appeared; around 1859, *Clarke's* (St. Louis) *Coin Chart* made its appearance; about 1860, *The Metropolitan Bank Note Reporter* (New York) put out the Metropolitan *Coin Book* as a supplement; and in 1862, *Preston's* (Detroit) *U. S. Bank Note and Commercial Reporter* offered a *Coin Chart Manual* as a supplement to their publication.

Appendix

WHILE many of these periodicals are known to the writer merely by name and few were found in the *Union List of Serials* (1943), a sufficient number came to light in libraries and historical societies throughout the country to warrant the compilation of this appendix. With the exception of the first four years that bank note reporters were published there is at least one monthly issue recorded in this appendix for each year from 1830 to 1866 inclusive. This record may be helpful to researchers and others in establishing the existence of a particular bank at a particular time and may furnish other information relating to banks and banking during that period.

This does not purport to be a complete list of all such periodicals in existence. It does, however, contain a reference to those found in the more important libraries and historical societies. In a few cases where a complete file is available for a particular calendar year, no reference has been made to individual issues for that particular year found in other places. It does not include any reference to issues held in private collections. A key to the dates of issues as well as a key to their location follows this compilation.

Following the schedule of bank note reporters is a list of the locations of copies of Hodges' Bank Note Safe-guards for the years 1857 to 1865 inclusive.

BANK NOTE REPORTERS

Year	Name and Place		Issues	Location
1830	Day	N. Y.	8	24
1831	Sylvester	N. Y.	3.6.7	1
1832	Sylvester	N. Y.	2	13
1832	Sylvester	N. Y.	10	14
1833	Bicknell	Phila.	5	4
1833	Day	N. Y.	6	28
1833	Sylvester	N. Y.	8	1
1833	Sylvester	N. Y.	12	25
1834	Bicknell	Phila.	4	20
1834	Bicknell	Phila.	7	21
1834	Bicknell	Phila.	11	3

Appendix

Year	Name and Place		Issues	Location
1835	Bicknell	Phila.	2	11
1835	Bicknell	Phila.	4.9.10	3
1836	Bicknell	Phila.	1	17
1836	Bicknell	Phila.	2.6.9	3
1836	Bicknell	Phila.	7.10.11.12	11
1837	Day	N. Y.	5	2
1837	Day	N. Y.	9	19
1837	Bicknell	Phila.	-5-	11
1837	Bicknell	Phila.	7	2
1837	Sylvester	N. Y.	12	1
1838	Clark	Boston	3.4.5.6	28
1838	Sylvester	N. Y.	10	19
1839	Clark	Boston	(M)	28
1839	Van Court	Phila.	-11-	21
1839	Sylvester	N. Y.	8	26
1840	Van Court	Phila.	(M)	21
1840	Clark	Boston	-9-	28
1840	Bicknell	Phila.	2	11
1840	Goodman	Cinn.	2	10
1840	Sylvester	N. Y.	3	16
1840	Day	N. Y.	4	22
1840	McIntyre	N. Y.	5.10	27
1840	Day	N. Y.	12	28
1841	Van Court	Phila.	(M)	21
1841	Goodman	Cinn.	2	10
1841	Day	N. Y.	11	28
1841	Clark	Boston	11	28
1842	Van Court	Phila.	(M)	21
1842	Charles	N. Y.	3.4	25
1842	Clark	Boston	3.5.11	28
1842	Thompson	N. Y.	9	3
1842	Sylvester	N. Y.	-5-	25
1843	Van Court	Phila.	(M)	21
1843	Bicknell	Phila.	1	17
1843	Bicknell	Phila.	9	27
1843	Bicknell	Phila.	11	17
1843	Willis	Boston	10.11.12	5
1843	Willis	Boston	11.12	28

Appendix

Year	Name and Place		Issues	Location
1844	Van Court	Phila.	(M)	21
1844	Willis	Boston	(M)	5
1844	Thompson	N. Y.	3	18
1844	Thompson	N. Y.	4.5	17
1845	Willis	Boston	(M)	5
1845	Willis	Boston	(M)	28
1845	Clark	Boston	4.6.12	28
1845	Bicknell	Phila.	11	17
1845	Clark	Boston	12	7
1845	Goodman	Cinn.	-6-	9
1845	Bicknell	Phila.	-10-	3
1845	Van Court	Phila.	-11-	21
1846	Van Court	Phila.	(M)	21
1846	Willis	Boston	(M)	5
1846	Goodman	Cinn.	(M)	9
1846	Thompson	N. Y.	3	17
1846	Bicknell	Phila.	5	28
1846	Goodman	Cinn.	6	10
1846	Sylvester	N. Y.	11	1
1846	Clark	Boston	11	7
1846	Bicknell	Phila.	12	17
1846	Taylor	N. Y.	12	28
1846	Bicknell	Phila.	-13-	3
1847	Van Court	Phila.	(M)	21
1847	Willis	Boston	(M)	5
1847	Taylor	N. Y.	2.6	23
1847	Charles	N. Y.	3	7
1847	Taylor	N. Y.	3.5.8.12	7
1847	Taylor	N. Y.	3.12	28
1847	Mearson	N. Y.	6	3
1847	Goodman	Cinn.	-6-	9
1847	Bicknell	Phila.	-18-	3
1848	Van Court	Phila.	(M)	21
1848	Willis	Boston	(M)	5
1848	Thompson	N. Y.	2	28
1848	Thompson	N. Y.	5	1
1848	Thompson	N. Y.	7	7
1848	Thompson	N. Y.	7	7

Appendix

Year	Name and Place		Issues	Location
1848	Taylor	N. Y.	8	27
1848	Goodman	Cinn.	9	15
1848	Thompson	N. Y.	10	3
1848	Sylvester	N. Y.	11	19
1848	Bicknell	Phila.	-17-	3
1849	Van Court	Phila.	(M)	21
1849	Willis	Boston	(M)	5
1849	Thompson	N. Y.	3	18
1849	Thompson	N. Y.	3	28
1849	Sylvester	N. Y.	9	2
1849	Bicknell	Phila.	-10-	3
1850	Van Court	Phila.	(M)	21
1850	Willis	Boston	(M)	5
1850	Bradley	Cinn.	2	10
1850	Bicknell	Phila.	-5-	3
1851	Van Court	Phila.	(M)	21
1851	Willis	Boston	(M)	5
1851	Thompson	N. Y.	1	18
1851	Bicknell	Phila.	1.3	3
1851	Thompson	N. Y.	-5-	28
1852	Van Court	Phila.	(M)	21
1852	Willis	Boston	(M)	5
1852	Thompson	N. Y.	-23-	28
1853	Van Court	Phila.	(M)	21
1853	Willis	Boston	(M)	5
1853	Sheldon	Chic.	7	8
1853	Thompson	N. Y.	-19-	28
1854	Van Court	Phila.	(M)	21
1854	Thompson	N. Y.	6	1
1854	Lord	Cinn.	7	16
1854	Thompson	N. Y.	8	27
1854	Willis	Boston	(9)	5
1854	Thompson	N. Y.	-19-	28
1855	Van Court	Phila.	(M)	21
1855	Thompson	N. Y.	12	3
1855	Thompson	N. Y.	-18-	28
1856	Van Court	Phila.	(M)	21
1856	Thompson	N. Y.	6	28

Appendix

Year	Name and Place		Issues	Location
1856	Thompson	N. Y.	8	28
1857	Thompson	N. Y.	(W)	27
1857	Van Court	Phila.	(M)	21
1857	Lord	Cinn.	2	28
1858	Van Court	Phila.	(M)	21
1858	Thompson	N. Y.	6	3
1858	Thompson	N. Y.	12	1
1858	Lee	Buff.	-6-	6
1859	Thompson	N. Y.	(W)	27
1859	Brown	Detroit	-25-	12
1859	Lee	Buff.	-45-	6
1860	Thompson	N. Y.	1	28
1861	Hodges	N. Y.	-19-	3
1862	Nicholas	N. Y.	1	19
1862	Hodges	N. Y.	-10-	3
1863	Metrop.	N. Y.	8	23
1863	Nicholas	N. Y.	9	19
1863	Hodges	N. Y.	-10-	3
1864	Thompson	N. Y.	1	28
1864	Nicholas	N. Y.	1.2	19
1864	Thompson	N. Y.	2	28
1864	Preston	Detroit	3	12
1864	Hodges	N. Y.	-9-	3
1865	Thompson	N. Y.	10	28
1865	Hodges	N. Y.	-11-	3
1866	Imlay & Bick.	Phila.	1	17
1866	Hodges	N. Y.	1.2.3.4	3
1866	Thompson	N. Y.	-8-	18

KEY TO ISSUES OF BANK NOTE REPORTERS

1. Numbers 1 to 12, either singly or separated by a period or periods, indicate the month or months of issue as:
   1, January; 2, February; 3, March; 6.10, June and October; 2.4.8, February, April, and August.
2. A number shown in this manner -14- indicates fourteen different issues in the particular year.
3. (W) Weekly issues for the entire year.
4. (M) Monthly issues for the entire year.

Appendix

KEY TO LOCATIONS OF BANK NOTE REPORTERS

1. New York State Library, Albany, New York.
2. University of Michigan, Ann Arbor, Michigan.
3. Baker Library, Harvard University Graduate School of Business Administration, Boston, Massachusetts.
4. Massachusetts Historical Society, Boston, Massachusetts.
5. The Public Library of the City of Boston, Massachusetts.
6. Buffalo Historical Society, Buffalo, New York.
7. Harvard College Library, Cambridge, Massachusetts.
8. Chicago Historical Society, Chicago, Illinois.
9. Cincinnati Public Library, Cincinnati, Ohio.
10. Historical and Philosophical Society of Ohio, Cincinnati, Ohio.
11. The Western Reserve Historical Society, Cleveland, Ohio.
12. The Public Library (Burton Historical Collection), Detroit, Michigan.
13. Duke University Library, Durham, North Carolina.
14. State Library and Museum, Harrisburg, Pennsylvania.
15. Indiana State Library, Indianapolis, Indiana.
16. State Historical Society, Madison, Wisconsin.
17. Rutgers University Library, New Brunswick, New Jersey.
18. The New-York Historical Society, New York, New York.
19. The New York Public Library, New York, New York.
20. American Philosophical Society, Philadelphia, Pennsylvania.
21. Library Company of Philadelphia, Pennsylvania.
22. Westerly Public Library, Westerly, Rhode Island.
23. The Essex Institute, Salem, Massachusetts.
24. Henry E. Huntington Library and Art Gallery, San Marino, California.
25. Union College Library, Schenectady, New York.
26. University of Illinois Library, Urbana, Illinois.
27. The Library of Congress, Washington, D. C.
28. American Antiquarian Society, Worcester, Massachusetts.

Appendix

HODGES' BANK NOTE SAFE-GUARD

Year	Edition	Location
1857	- O -	The American Numismatic Society, New York, New York.
1858	3rd Quarterly	Baker Library, Boston, Massachusetts.
1858	4th Quarterly	Library of Congress, Washington, D. C.
1859	1st Quarterly	Columbia University, Business Library, New York, New York.
1859	1st Quarterly	Baker Library, Boston, Massachusetts.
1860	4th Quarterly	Baker Library, Boston, Massachusetts.
1860	4th Quarterly	The American Numismatic Society, New York, New York.
1861	- O -	Baker Library, Boston, Massachusetts.
1861	Revised	Baker Library, Boston, Massachusetts.
1862	Revised	Library of Congress, Washington, D. C.
1862	- O -	Essex Institute, Salem, Massachusetts.
1863	Revised	Massachusetts State Library, Boston, Massachusetts.
1863	- O -	Library of Congress, Washington, D. C.
1864	- O -	The American Numismatic Society, New York, New York.
1865	- O -	Massachusetts State Library, Boston, Massachusetts.
1865	- O -	Baker Library, Boston, Massachusetts.

Bibliography

Books and Pamphlets

An Appeal to the Legislature For an Ounce of Prevention. Boston: 1855.

Barrere, Albert, and Leland, Charles G. *A Dictionary of Slang, Jargon & Cant.* 2 vols. Edinburgh: 1889.

Bartlett, John Russell. *Dictionary of Americanisms.* 4th ed. Boston: 1877.

Berkey, William A. *The Money Question. The Legal Tender Paper Money System of the United States.* 2d ed. Grand Rapids: Hart, 1878.

Bryan, Alfred Cookman. "History of State Banking in Maryland," *Johns Hopkins University Studies in History and Politics,* Ser. XVII, Nos. 1, 2, and 3 (1899).

Coins and Currency of the United States, Office of the Secretary of the Treasury, June 30, 1947.

Craigie, W. A. *Dictionary of American Language on Historical Principles.* 4 vols. Chicago: 1938-1944.

De Vere, M. Schele. *Americanisms, The English of the New World.* New York: 1872.

Dye's Coin Encyclopaedia. Philadelphia: 1883.

Facts about Paper Money. [U. S.] Treasury Department. Washington: January, 1948.

Fearon, Henry Bradshaw. *A Narrative of a Journey Through The Eastern and Western States of America.* 3d ed. London: 1819.

Fowler, Wm. W. *Ten Years in Wall Street.* Hartford: 1870.

Francis, John. *History of the Bank of England.* 3d ed. London: 1848.

French, J. H. *Gazetteer of the State of New York.* Syracuse: 1860.

Gilbert & Dean. *The Only Sure Guide to Bank Bills.* Boston: 1806.

Gouge, William M. *The Journal of Banking.* Philadelphia: 1841.

Greeley, Horace. *Recollections of a Busy Life.* New York: 1872.

The History of the Little Frenchman and His Bank Notes. Philadelphia: 1815.

Jones, Breckinridge. "One Hundred Years of Banking in Missouri, 1820-1920," *The Missouri Historical Review.* Vol. XV (January, 1921).

Kenny, Daniel J. *The American Newspaper Directory and Record of the Press.* New York: 1861.

Knox, John Jay. *A History of Banking in the United States.* New York: 1903.

Bibliography

Landauer Trade Cards, The New-York Historical Society, New York, N. Y.

Larson, Henrietta M. *Jay Cooke, Private Banker*. Cambridge: 1936.

Livingston's (John) *Law Register For 1852*. New York.

Lowndes Letters to Calhoun. New York: 1843.

Lyell, Charles. *Travels in North America in the Years 1841–2*. Vol. I, New York: 1852.

Meigs, William M. *The Life of Thomas Hart Benton*. Philadelphia: 1904.

Merritt, Fred D. "The Early History of Banking in Iowa," *University of Iowa Bulletin*, No. 15 (June, 1900).

Ormsby, W. L. *A Description of the Present System of Bank Note Engraving*. New York: 1852.

Partridge, Eric. *A Dictionary of Slang and Unconventional English*. 2d ed. London: 1938.

Patchin, Sydney A. "Banking in Minnesota," *Minnesota History Bulletin*, II (August, 1917).

Perkins, Jacob. *The Permanent Stereotype Steel Plate*. Newburyport, Massachusetts: 1806.

The Philadelphia National Bank, A Century's Record 1803–1903. Philadelphia: 1903.

Phillips, Jr., Henry. *Historical Sketches of the Paper Money of the American Colonies*. First Series, Roxbury, Massachusetts: 1865.

Platt, Edmund. *The Eagle's History of Poughkeepsie*. Poughkeepsie: 1905.

Preston, Howard H. *History of Banking in Iowa*. Iowa City: 1922.

Scroggs, William O. *A Century of Banking Progress*. New York: 1924.

Sherman, Hoyt. "Early Banking in Iowa," *Annals of Iowa*, 3d Series (Des Moines, April, 1901), V. No. 1.

Sumner, William Graham. *A History of Banking in the United States*. New York: 1896.

Thornton, Richard H. *An American Glossary*, Philadelphia: 1912.

Valentine's Manual of Old New York. No. 5, New Series, 1921.

Vowles, H. P. and M. W. "A Study in American Ingenuity and Intrepid Pioneering," *Mechanical Engineering*, November, 1931.

Weiss, Harry B. "Mahlon Day," *Bulletin of The New York Public Library*, XLV (December, 1941).

White, Horace. *Money and Banking*. Fifth Edition, New York: 1914.

Bibliography

Newspapers and Magazines

The Albany (New York) Argus.
The American (New York).
American Banker (New York).
The American Daily Advertiser (Philadelphia).
The Bankers' Magazine and Statistical Register (New York), 1849-1894.
Boston Daily Traveller.
The Boston Gazette and Weekly Republican Journal.
The Brooklyn Eagle, and Kings County Democrat.
Cincinnati Gazette.
Commercial Advertiser of New York.
The Congressional Globe.
Congressional Record.
The Daily Advertiser (New York).
The Daily Guardian (Paterson, New Jersey).
The Falls City Register (Paterson, New Jersey).
Gazette of the United States (Philadelphia).
Laurensville Herald (Laurens, North Carolina).
Litchfield Enquirer (Litchfield, Connecticut).
The Merchants' Magazine and Commercial Review (New York), 1839-1870.
Minnesota Pioneer.
Missouri (St. Louis) Monitor.
New York Advertiser.
New York Evening Post.
New York Express.
New York Gazette and General Advertiser.
New York Herald.
New York Journal of Commerce.
New York Packet.
New-York Shipping and Commercial List.
The New York Tribune.
Niles' Weekly Register (Baltimore).
The Pittsburgh Dispatch.
The Public Ledger (Philadelphia).
St. Augustine (Florida) News.
The Weekly Herald (New York).

Index

Abbot, A., cashier, City Trust and Banking Co., 69
Adams, Francis Granger, 92, 93, 115, 117, 118, 143
Adams, Platt, 92; as publisher of Thompson's reporter, 88
Adams, Robert, Jr., member of Congress, 55
Adams' *Bank Note Descriptive List*, 143
Agents, traveling, 8
Alabama, 15, 37; lotteries in behalf of, 125
Albany Argus, 67
Albany Bank Bills, counterfeit, 13
Allen, Jr., J., cashier, The Gloucester Bank, 23, 24
Allen, Moses, 3; Solomon, 3; S. and M., 3
Almanac, miniature, published by Mahlon Day, 98
Altered bank notes, 18-23, 27-28, 32-37; definition, 16; detection, 20; method of making, 20, 33, 34
Altered plates, 20-21
American, The (New York City), 7
American Bank Note Company, 149
American Banker, 90
American Book of Coins (Bicknell's), 153
Andover (Massachusetts) Bank, 19
Appellations, Bank Note, 65-70; *see also* Paper currency
Applegate, Mr., printer, 49
Arnold, Joseph, 102
Autographical Counterfeit Detector (Thompson's), 150-152

Backs of notes, ornamentations on, 30
Baker, Crane and Day, 100
Baltimore and Ohio Rail Road notes, 45
Baltimore bank note, 5
Bang, J. N., 112
Bank Bills, The Only Sure Guide to, 25, 26
Bank charters, granting of, 59
Bank Mirror, 131
Bank note alterations, *see* Altered Bank Notes
Bank Note & Commercial Reporter, The, 85

Bank Note Appellations, 65-70; *see also* Paper currency
Bank Note Counterfeits and Alterations, in 1853, 32
Bank note currency in New York, 32
Bank Note Descriptive List (Chicago), 143
Bank Note Descriptive Lists, 142
Bank Note Detector (St. Louis), 140
"Bank Note Exchange," 7; table of, 97
"Bank Note List and Insurance Reporter" (New York), 108
Bank note lists, 1, 6, 16, 41, 44, 94
Bank Note Mirror (Pittsburgh), 137
Bank note plates, making of, by Bureau of Engraving and Printing, 31; making of, by Perkins' process, 31
Bank Note Rates of Exchange and Counterfeit Detector (Philadelphia), 131
Bank note register, of the Bank of the State of Georgia, 22
Bank Note Register and Counterfeit Detector, Buffalo, 114, 115, 131
Bank Note Register and Detector of Counterfeits (Gwynne & Day's), 104, 115, 149
Bank Note Reporter (Montreal), 125
Bank Note Reporter (Pittsburgh), 137
Bank note reporters, key to locations, 154-159; subscription rates, 42, 84, 100
Bank Note Reporters and Counterfeit Detectors, 41-58, 78-140
Bank note tables, 6, 9, 68
Bank of Albany, N. Y., 13
Bank of Clinton, Michigan, 43
Bank of Constantine, Michigan, 43
Bank of England, counterfeit notes of, 10; one pound note, 29
Bank of Illinois, 116
Bank of Macomb County, Michigan, 43
Bank of Massachusetts, Boston, 1
Bank of Morgan, Georgia, 19
Bank of New York, 1, 12, 17
Bank of North America, Philadelphia, 1, 11, 12
Bank of Redemption, Boston; *see* National Bank of Redemption

166 Index

Bank of River Raisin, 43
Bank of St. Clair, Michigan, 43
Bank of Tecumseh, Michigan, 43
Bank of the State of Georgia, 21, 22
Bank of the United States, 12, 21, 44; Boston branch, counterfeit bills in circulation, 28; New York branch, 80; Savannah branch, 21; Second, 59, 79; v. Bank of the State of Georgia, 21
Bank of Washtenaw, Michigan, 43
Bank of West Union, 44
Bank of Ypsilanti, Michigan, 43
"Bankable funds," 75
Bankers' Magazine and Statistical Register (New York), 139
Banking and currency in Cincinnati, 5
Banking Law of 1838, New York General, 68
Beach, cashier, Newark Banking and Insurance Company, 17
Beach, Moses Y., owner of the *Sun*, 86
Bennett, James Gordon, 47
Benton, Col. Thomas H., 61, 70-71, 138
"Bentonian Currency," a copper token, 72
Benton's Bullets, 69, 70
Benton's Mint-Drops, 70
Bentonville Bank, Illinois, 56
Bepler & Co., 122
Bepler's Bank Notes-Lists (Cincinnati), printed in German, 122
Bergen Iron Works, 76, 77
Bicknell, Charles P., 128
Bicknell, Robert T., 125-128, 132
Bicknell's *American Book of Coins*, 153
Bicknell's Boston Edition, 114
Bicknell's Counterfeit Detector and Bank Note List (Pamphlet Edition), described, 114, 126
Bicknell's Counterfeit Detector, and Pennsylvania Reporter of Bank Notes, 126
Bicknell's Counterfeit Detector, and Pennsylvania Reporter of Bank Notes, Broken Banks, Stocks, etc., 125
Bicknell's reporter, 48, 129, 137, 138; prospectus of, 125
Bicknell's Reporter, Counterfeit Detector, and General Prices Current, 126
Bicknell's Reporter, Counterfeit Detector, and Philadelphia Prices Current, 126
Bicknell's Reporter, Counterfeit Detector, and Prices Current, 126
Black money, 65

Blondell, Charles, 92
Blow, to, 50, 58
Blue pup money, 65, 68
Blue stamp, on back of notes, 68
Bluebacks, 65, 68
Bobtail notes, 65, 74, 75
Boston, reporters published in, 111-114
Boston Daily Traveller, 113
Bradford's *New-York Gazette*, 11
Bradley & Co., M. A., 121
Bradley & Co's Cincinnati Counterfeit Detector and Bank Note Reporter, 122
Brewster, Abel, bank note plate engraver, 32, 39
Bribing of publishers, 57
Brindle-pup, 65, 68, 75
Broken bank notes, 25
Broken Bank Notes *vs.* Obsolete Notes, 25
Brokers, 1, 2, 8, 9; *see also* Note brokers and note shavers; bill, 8; in important trading centers, 1; mercenary, 47; merchandise, 2
Brokers' advertisements, 2-3, 6
Brooklyn Eagle, and Kings County Democrat, 68
Brown, J., 124
Brown's Bank Note Reporter (Detroit), 124, 144
Brown's Descriptive List of Genuine Bank Notes (Detroit), 143
Buckeye, 70
Buffalo Historical Society, 115
Bureau of Engraving and Printing, 30
Burgwyn, Col., a national bank examiner, 64

Cairo swindling shop, 71, 72
Calhoun County Bank, Michigan, 43
Calhoun, John C., U. S. Senator from South Carolina, 44
Camp, H. H., president, Milwaukee Trust Company, 52
Canada, 13, 106; wildcats of, 73
Canal companies, notes of, 25
Cape May, New Jersey, 76
Carpet-bags and Carpet-baggers, 61, 63-64
Catamount, third quality Michigan money, 68
Cataract City Bank, Paterson, New Jersey, 142
Centinel, The (Boston), 26

Index

Central Bank of Alabama at Montgomery, 19
Central Bank of Cherry Valley, New York, 18
Central Bank of Hightstown, New Jersey, 18
Central Bank of (Nashville) Tennessee, 18, 19
Change Alley, 71
Charles, Edmund, 93, 96
Charles & Co., Edmund, 95
Charles & Leonori's New York Bank Note List, Counterfeit Detector, Wholesale Prices Current, and Commercial Journal, 96
Charles & Leonori's (Late Taylor's) Signature Examiner, 152
Charles & Son's, Edmund, New York Bank Note List, Counterfeit Detector, Wholesale Prices Current and Weekly Journal of Financial News, 95
Charles, McIntire & Co., 95
Charles, McIntyre & Co., 93, 94, 95
Charleston, S. C., 116
Chase National Bank of the City of New York, 93
Cheapside, 71, 72
Check letters, on notes of the Bank of the State of Georgia, 22
Cherry Valley, New York, 18
Chicago, 75, 108; reporters published in, 116-120
Chicago Bank Note List, 117, 118, 143
Chicago Tribune, 74
Church & Co., 119
Cincinnati, 5, 50; reporters published in, 120-124
Cincinnati Counterfeit Detector and Bank Note Reporter, 121
Cincinnati Gazette, 57
Cincinnati Safety Fund Bank Note Reporter, 123
Circuit Court of Georgia, 22
City Trust and Banking Co., New York, 68
Civil War, 66, 74
Clapp, Fuller & Browne's Bank Note Reporter and Counterfeit Detector (Boston), 113
Clark, Enoch W., 139
Clark & Brother, E. W., 139, 145
Clark & Co., J. W., 112

Clark's Counterfeit Detector (St. Louis), 139
Clark's Monetype (St. Louis), 145
Clark's New-England Bank Note List (Boston), 112
Clark's New-England Bank Note List and Counterfeit Bill Detector (Boston), 112
Clarke, Robert L., 139, 145
Clarke's Coin Chart (St. Louis), 153
Clarke's Descriptive List of Genuine Bank Notes, 145
Cohn, A., 107
Coin Chart Manuals, 52, 152
Colonial notes, 2, 65
Commercial Bank of Perth Amboy, New Jersey, 20
Commercial Banks, 20
Condit, president, Newark Banking and Insurance Company, 17
Confederate States, notes of, 25, 68
Connecticut Bank Commissioners, 51
Continental & State Certificates, 2
Continental currency, 11, 66
Continental State money, 65
Coon box, 71, 72
Copper token, Benton, 72
Corkery, Charles, 69
Corncracker, 70
Counterfeit detectors, 41-58, 78-140
Counterfeit notes, branding of, 17; crossing of, 17
Counterfeiter's art, examples of the, 17
Counterfeiters and Counterfeiting, 10-40
Counterfeiters and Their Tricks, A Lecture on, 36
Covington & Danville Plank Road Company, 73
Crackee, 74; jr., 74
Crane, Stephen M., 100
Crane, William E., 100
Crossing, counterfeit notes, 14, 17; genuine notes, 14
Crow scalp certificates, 62
Cullender, C. D., 57
Currency tray, description of an old, 75

Davis, Thomas, counterfeiter, 15
Davis, W. F., a detector of counterfeit notes, 114
Day, Clarence S., 104
Day, Mahlon, 41, 96-101, 125
Day and Turner, 97

Day's Bank Note Table, and Expose of Counterfeit Notes, 101
Day's New York Bank Note List, Counterfeit Detecter & Price Current, 97
Day's New-York Bank Note List, Counterfeit Detecter and Price Current, 17; description of contents, 99
Day's New-York Miniature Almanac, description of, 98
Day's reporter, 137, 138
Delaware and Hudson Bank, Ocean County, N. J., 76, 77
Demand notes of 1861, 68
Demi-notes, 6
DeMott, George, 96
Denominational designs on paper currency, 40
Describer of Genuine Bank Notes (White's), 143
Description of Genuine Bank Notes (Kennedy's), 149
Descriptive List of Genuine Bank Notes (Adams'), 117
Descriptive Register of Genuine Bank Notes (Gwynne & Day's), 148
Detroit, detectors published in, 124
Dickinson & Co., 112
Discount on bank notes, 1-9, 45, 77, 101
District of Columbia, 106
Dodge, William Earl, a New York merchant, 45
Drexel & Co., 129, 130
Dye, John S., 36, 51, 102-103, 123, 137, 145-146
Dye's *Bank Bulletin,* 103
Dye's *Bank Mirror,* 145
Dye's *Bank Mirror and Illustrated Counterfeit Detector* (Cincinnati), 102, 123
Dye's *Bank Note Plate Delineator,* 145
Dye's *Counterfeit Detector and Universal Bank Note Gazetteer* (Cincinnati), 102, 123
Dye's *Delineator,* 145-147
Dye's *Gold and Silver Coin Chart Manual,* 153
Dye's *Government Counterfeit Detector,* 103
Dye's *Wall Street Broker,* 103

Early Banks and Bank Note Lists, 1

Eastern, and southern bills, 3; funds, 136; money, 89; Penn., notes, 75; States, 13; wild-cat bankers, 89; wild-cat money, 89
English traveler, experiences of an, 5, 43
Engraving bills, cost of, 57
Erie, Pennsylvania, 74
Erie & Kalamazoo Railroad Bank, 43
Essex Bank of Salem, Massachusetts, 27, 28
Exploded banks, 16
Exporter and Banking Circular (New York), 108

"false Jersey money," 11
Farmers' & Mechanics' Bank of Detroit, 43
Farmers' and Mechanics' Bank of Hartford, 37
Farmers' and Mechanics' Bank of St. Joseph, 43
Farmers' Bank, Wickford, R. I., 19
Farmers' Banks, 19, 20
Feld and Lare, 137
Fillmore, Millard, 60
Financial troubles of 1837, 46
First National Bank of the City of New York, 92
Fleming, J. A., cashier, Central Bank of Tennessee, 19
Forged notes, 42
Foster, A. S., exchange broker, 100
Foster's (late Day's) *New-York Counterfeit Recorder and Bank Note Table,* 100
Fractional currency, amount outstanding, June 30, 1877, 66
Fredericktown, 45
"Free Banking," 59, 61, 67, 68
French, notes described in, 103
French, Samuel, 106
French visitor, a, 3
Frogtown bank, 63, 64

Galena Branch, Illinois State Bank, 43
General Counterfeit Detector (Cincinnati), 123
Genuine notes, crossing of, 14
Georgia, wildcats of, 73
Gerhard, Frederich, 103
German, notes described in, 103

Index 169

German Bank Note Reporter (New York), 103
Gilbert and Dean, 26-28, 41
Globe Bank of New York, 69
Gloucester (Massachusetts) Bank *v.* Salem Bank, 23-25
Gold coins, known as Benton's mint drops, 71
Goodman, Charles, 120
Goodman, T. S., 121
Goodman & Co., H. H., 120
Goodman & Co., T. S., 120
Greeley, Horace, 110
Greeley & Story, 110
Green Bay Bank, 43
Greenbacks, 65, 68
Groom & Co., Thomas, 112
Guide to Bank Bills, The Only Sure, 25, 26
Gwynne, John A., 104
Gwynne & Day, 104, 149
Gwynne & Day's *Descriptive Register*, 148

"Hard money," advocate, Benton a, 70
Hartford, Indiana, bogus bank at, 57
Hightstown, N. J., 18
Historical Magazine, 74
Hodges, Daniel Milton, 105, 148
Hodges, Edwin M., 105, 148
Hodges, J. Tyler, 105, 144, 146, 148
Hodges' *American Bank Note Safe-Guard*, 148
Hodges' *Bank Note Safe-Guard*, errors in bank names, 147; where found, by years and editions, 160
Hodges' *Coin Chart Manual*, 106
Hodges' *Genuine Bank Notes of America*, 144
Hodges' *Genuine Notes of America*, 106
Hodges' *Gold and Silver Coin Chart Manual*, 153
Hodges' *Journal of Finance and Bank Note Reporter* (New York), 105, 106
Hodges' *New Bank Note Safe-Guard*, 106, 146, 148
Holes through bank notes, 46
Hoosier Tame Cat, 70
Houghton, E. L., cashier, Litchfield Bank, 51
Hubbard, H. H., president, Central Bank of Tennessee, 19
"hush money" paid to publishers—Dye, Monroe, and Taylor, 51

Illinois, bank notes, 75, 139; banks in, 70, 136; stump-tail notes of, 73
Illinois River Bank, Peru City, Illinois, 73
Illinois State Bank, Galena Branch, 43
Imlay, Charles G., 128
Imlay & Bicknell, 125
Imlay's & Bicknell's Bank Note Reporter (Philadelphia), 128, 131
Indiana, banks in, 70, 136; notes, 75; red dogs of, 73
Iowa, 69; paper money in, 42
Iowa News, 69

Jackson, Andrew, 19
Jacksonville Bank, Florida, 47, 48, 50; charter annulled, 49; shin-plasters of, 50
Jansen, B., 3
Jersey money, false, 11
Jersey Paper Money, 2
Johnson Bros. & Co., 122
Johnson, Phillips and Company, 140
Jones & Co., S., 136
Journal of Finance, J. Monroe, proprietor of (New York), 105
Journal of Finance & Bank Reporter (New York), 105
June, D. F., 107

Kaple & Co., J. H., Detroit, 124
Kelley, James E., 77
Kelley, Wlliam D., member of Congress, 63
Kendrick, George W., 119
Kennedy and Brother, Pittsburgh, 136, 149, 150
Kennedy Review Office, 149
Kennedy's Bank Note Review and Fac Simile Counterfeit Detector (Pittsburgh), 137
Kennedy's Descriptive List, 149
Kennedy's Fac Simile Counterfeit Note Detector, 150
Kennedy's Fac Simile, Ein Supplement Zu ihrem Vereinigte Staaten Banknoten Kenner, 150
Kentucky, 70; banks, 136; money, 45, 75; "Rags" of, 73

Index

Kinderhook, 20

Lake Erie & River Raisin R. R. Co., 43
Lakewood, New Jersey, 76
Langdon, Hawes & Co., 123
Lawrence & Cos'., L. S., Bank Note List (New York), 106
Lawrence & Co.'s, L. S., Bank Note List, New England Edition, 113, 114
Lee, Edward L., 114
Lee, John R., 114, 116
Lee, Martin, 7
Lee, William W., 86, 150
Lee's Bank Note Register and Counterfeit Detecter (Buffalo), 115
Legal tender, bounty certificates as, 66; notes 68; wildcat certificates as, 62
Leonori, Lewis J., 96
Leonori's New York Bank Note Reporter, Counterfeit Detector & Wholesale Prices Current, 96
Libby, John, 132
Libel action against John Thompson, 90
License, fee, 9; to purchase notes, 8
Lincoln and Kennebeck Bank of Wiscasset, Maine, 27
Litchfield (Connecticut) Bank, 51
Lord, Thomas R., 88
Lord & Co., Thos. R., 122
Lord, T. W., 121, 140
Lord & Co., T. W., 122
Lord's Detector (St. Louis), 123, 140
Lord's Detector and Bank Note Reporter (Cincinnati), 122
Lord's Detector and Bank Note Vignette Describer (Cincinnati), 88, 122
Lord's Detector Office (St. Louis), 140
Lotteries, under state supervision, 94
Lottery and exchange offices, 2, 3, 5, 109
Louisville, 50; notes, 5
Lyell, Charles, 43

Maine Bank at Portland, 28
Manson, J. B., president, City Trust and Banking Co., 69
Manufacturers' Bank, Hartford, Ind., 57
Manufacturers' Bank, Ulster, New York, 47, 48
Manufacturers' Bank, Ware, Mass., 38
Marks, to detect frauds, 22
Maryland, 8, 45; notes, 75
Maryland Journal, 65

Massachusetts, bills in, 28
Mayer, Alexander, 119
McCammon, Jr., W., 120
McElroy, Solon, 120
McElroy's Bank Note Reporter (Chicago), 120
McIntire & Co., 95
McIntyre, Archibald, 83, 93; services to the State of New York, 94
McIntyre & Co., Charles, 93
Mearson, George, 107
Mearson's United States Bank Note Reporter (New York), 107
Mendelson, L., 107
Mercantile Bank, Salem, Mass., 37
Merchants' Bank at Trenton, N. J., 91
Merchant's Recollections of Old New York, A Great, 45
Messenger, H. J., private banker, 104, 149
Metropolitan Bank Note Reporter (New York), 104, 149, 153
Metropolitan Coin Book, 153
Metropolitan National Bank Note Reporter (New York), 104, 149
Michigan, 65, 68, 74; bill, 37; banks in, 43; shinplasters of, 73
Miller, Matthew T., 128
Minnesota, 74
Mint Drops, Benton's, 72
Mississippi plan, 68
Missouri, 62, 66; banks in, 70; notes, 75; "Rags" of, 73
Missouri Monitor, 138
Mohawk Bank of Schenectady, N. Y., 4
Mohawk Valley Bank, Mohawk, New York, 67, 68, 151
Mongrel notes, 68
Monroe, "hush money" paid to, 51
Monroe, J., Charleston, S. C., 116
Monroe, James, 105
Monroe, John, 144
Monroe & Hodges, 105
Monroe's Descriptive List of Genuine Bank Notes (New York), 144
Monroe's Southern Banker (Charleston, S. C.), 116
Montgomery, Alabama, 124
Montgomery, Robert, 129
Montgomery's reporter (Philadelphia), 129
Montreal, Canada, 125

Index

Morgan, Captain, president, Jacksonville Bank, 49, 50
Morrison, E., 108, 115
Morrison and Company, E., 108, 111
Mt. Vernon, Ohio, bank at, 72

Nantucket Bank, 28
Nashville, Tenn., 18
National bank, establishment of a, 44
National Bank Act, V, 59, 92; see also National Banking System
National Bank Note Reporter (New York), 107
National Bank Note Reporter and Financial Gazette (New York), 107
National Bank of Paterson, New Jersey, 23
National Bank of Redemption, Boston, 17
National Bank Reporter (Pittsburgh), 137
National Banking System, 38
National Currency Bank of New York, 92; in liquidation, 93
National Journal of Finance (New York), 106
National Journal of Finance and Hodges' Bank Note Reporter (New York), 105
Nebraska, red dogs of, 73
New England, banks in, 27, 39; counterfeits in, 35; notes, 75
New England Edition, *L. S. Lawrence & Cos.' Bank Note List*, 106, 113
New Jersey Wildcats, Some, 76
New Orleans, The Battle of, 18, 19
"New Series," of paper currency issued in 1929, 39
New York, 39, 46, 68
New York American, 83
New York Bank Note List and Counterfeit Detecter, notice of publication, 98
New York Bank Note List, Counterfeit Detector, Wholesale Prices Current, and General Banking Statistic, 95
"New York Commercial Circular," 95
New York Herald, 49, 50, 74
New York Journal of Commerce, 68
New-York Loan Company, 69
New-York Shipping and Commercial List, description of contents, 97
New-York Telegraph, McIntyre's Bank Note List and Prices Current, 94
New-York Telegraph, M'Intyre's Gazette and General Advertiser, 93
New York Tribune, 47, 48, 88

Newark Banking and Insurance Company, 17
Nicholas & Co., A., 108
Nicholas, Anastasius, 107, 108
Nicholas, S., 17
Nicholas, Bowen & Co., 108
Nicholas' New York and Chicago Bank Note Reporter, 108
Nichols, D., 17 (note 19)
Nixon, J., president, Bank of North America, 12
Noah, Manuel, 2
North Carolina, 64
North Carolina, "Rags" of, 73
North-Western Bank Note and Counterfeit Detector (Chicago), 119
North Western Bank of Virginia, 45
North Western Money Reporter (Chicago), 119
Norwich (Connecticut) Bank, 27, 28
Note broker, the first, 2
Note brokers, 1, 8, 9; see also Brokers and note shavers
Note shavers, 5, 8
Notes, circulating, 1; see also Paper currency

Obsolete Notes, Broken Bank Notes vs., 25
Obsolete notes, defined, 25
Ocean Bank, 36, 37; at Bergen Iron Works, N. J., 76
Ohio, 7, 70; banks, 136; notes, 75
Ohio Life Insurance and Trust Company, Cincinnati, 48, 89; failure of, 87
Ongley, Wm. H., 120
Orr, J. W., 151
Oswego & Indiana Plank Road Company, 73
Owl creek, 71
Owl Creek Bank, Mount Vernon, Ohio, 72

Page, Horatio, 139
Panic in 1841, 67; in 1857, 87
Panoramic display of counterfeits, 36
Panther bounty certificates, legal tender for taxes, 62
Paper currency; see altered bank notes, bank bills, black money, blue pup money, bluebacks, bobtail notes, brindle-pup, broken bank notes, buckeye, canal companies, catamount, Colonial notes,

172   *Index*

Confederate States, Continental currency, Corn-cracker, crow scalp certificates, crackee, crackee, jr., demand notes, demi-notes, "eastern and southern bills," Eastern money, "false Jersey money," forged notes, fractional currency, genuine notes, greenbacks, Hoosier Tame Cat, Jersey Paper Money, legal tender notes, mongrel notes, "New Series," obsolete notes, panther certificates, Perkins' note, plank road, post notes, postage stamps, postal currency, Puke, rag tag, "rags," railroad notes, raised notes, red back notes, red dog currency and notes, red horse notes, red money, reduced size currency, shinplasters, silver certificates, Southern States notes, spurious notes, State bank notes, stolen notes, stump-tail, Sucker, thirty shilling bills, three pound bills, tickets, twelve shilling bills, uncurrent bills, wildcat certificates, wildcat notes, wolf certificates

Par funds, choice, 75
Paterson (N. J.) Bank, 17
Pennsylvania, banks, 136; wildcats of, 73
Pennsylvania Legislature, 11
Perkins, Jacob, 29-32
Perkins' note, 24
Perkins' Stereotype Steel Plate, 28-30, 32
Perkins' Transfer Press, description of, 30
Peterson, C. J., 130
Peterson, T. B., 129
Peterson & Brothers, T. B., 129
Peterson Magazine, The, 130
Peterson's Complete Coin Book (Philadelphia), 153
Peterson's Philadelphia Counterfeit Detector and Bank Note List, 19, 53, 130
Peterson's detector, 20; described, 129
Phelps, James N., 105
Philadelphia, 5, 11, 13, 36, 43; bank notes, 2; bank note reporter, 68; imprint, 102; reporters published in, 125
Philadelphia Counterfeit Detector and Bank Note List, 134
Philadelphia Reporter, Counterfeit Detector and Prices Current, 133
Philadelphia Reporter, Counterfeit Detector, Philadelphia Prices Current, and General Advertiser, 132
Phillips, Bezaleel W., 119

Phillips' North Western Money Reporter and Insurance Journal (Chicago), 119
"pioneer" counterfeiter, 15
Pittsburgh, 5, 135; reporters published in, 135-137
"plank road," 73
Planters' and Merchants' Bank, Huntsville, Alabama, 21
Planters' Bank of Alabama, 37
Planters' Bank of Tennessee, 37
Pontiac, Michigan, 37
Poole, Isaac A., 119
Post notes, 69
Postage stamps, as currency, 66
Postal currency, 66
Presbury & Company, 138
Presbury & Company, George G., 138
Presbury and Company's Counterfeit Detector (St. Louis), 138
Preston, David, 124
Preston & Co., David, 124
Preston, Willard & Kean, 124
Preston's Bank Note Reporter (Detroit), 124
Preston's Coin Chart Manual (Detroit), 153
Preston's Descriptive List (Detroit), 144
Preston's Detroit and Chicago Bank Note Reporter, 124, 144
Preston's U. S. Bank Note and Commercial Reporter (Detroit), 153
Private marks on bank notes, 22
Prouty, Libby and Prouty, 133
Providence Bank, Providence, R. I., 38
Puffing, 47, 48
Puke, 70

Rag tag, 65, 75
"Rags," 65;—"Rags" of Kentucky, 73; of Missouri, 73; of North Carolina, 73; of Virginia, 73
Railroads, notes of, 25
Raised notes, 16, 21-23, 35, 38, 41
Ranson, Lewis E., 93
Rawdon, Wright & Hatch, 37
Rawdon, Wright, Hatch and Edson, 19
Red back notes, 65, 67, 68
Red Dog, first quality Michigan money, 68;—Red dog banks, 68;—Red-dog currency, 56, 65, 67, 68, 69, 71, 73, 74;—Red dogs, of Indiana, 73;—of Nebraska, 73

Index

Red horse notes, 65, 68, 75
Red money, 65
Redemption of notes, 25, 76-77; three days' grace in New Jersey, 76
Reduced size currency, 39; counterfeiting of, 12
Reed, Jun., Jacob, 2
Reed, Silas K., 118
Retired banks, 142
Rhode Island, banks in, 89
Rhodes, Charles C., 128
River Raison Bank, Munroe, Michigan, 48
Rogers, Linton, 136
Rumsey, first owner, Litchfield bank, 51

Saddle-bags; see Carpet-bags and Carpet-baggers
"saddle-bag" banks, 63
St. Augustine (Florida) *News*, 49
St. Louis, reporters published in, 137-140
St. Louis Bank Note Reporter, 139
St. Louis Daily Morning Herald, 73
Salem (Massachusetts) Bank, 23-24, 27
Savannah, Georgia, 3, 21
Second Bank of the United States, 59, 79; see also Bank of the United States
Secret marks on bank notes, 22
Shavers, note, 5, 8
Shaving of bank notes, 45
Sheldon, Reuben, 117, 118
Sheldon & Company, 117
Sheldon's North American Bank Note Detector and Commercial Reporter (Chicago), 42, 117, 118
Sherman, Major Hoyt, 51, 75, 93
Sherman's Money Drawer, 74
Shin-plaster, a cant term, 66
Shin-plasters, 44, 65; Good Intent, 45;— Shinplasters, of Michigan, 73; of the Jacksonville Bank, 50; used to bandage a wounded leg, 66
Shoe and Leather Bank, New York, libel action against John Thompson, 90, 91
Sibbet & Co., E., 135
Sibbet & Jones, 136
Sibbet's Bank Note Review and Counterfeit Detector (Pittsburgh), 136
Sibbet's Western Review and Counterfeit Detector, 136
Sibbet's Western Review Counterfeit List and Monthly Report of the Currency and Markets, 136

Signatures, fictitious, 27
Silver Certificates, 40, 75
Silver coins, subsidiary, disappeared from circulation, 66
Skunktown bank, 64
Sloane, C. S., 96, 151
Smith, John T., 101
Smith & Co., John T., 99
Smith, Richard, 123
Smithfield Union Bank of Rhode Island, 28
Snyder, Benjamin, 77
Snyder, John L., 77
Somes, John, president, The Gloucester Bank, 23
Southern Bank of (Bainbridge) Georgia, 19
Southern States, 12; bonds of, 74; notes of, 25
Southern traveler, a, experience with paper currency, 44
Spanish dollars, cut, 5, 6
Spear, John J., 114
Specie, 6, 9, 65; and current funds, 67
Spinner, Francis E., cashier, Mohawk (N. Y.) Valley Bank, 67, 151
"Spurious Currency," comments regarding, 43
Spurious notes, 14, 15, 16, 17, 37, 41, 43
State bank notes, liability for redemption of, 25; 10% tax on, 77
State Bank of Indiana, counterfeits on, 42
State Bank of Michigan, 43
State Bank of Missouri, 37
Stereotype plate; see Perkins' Stereotype Steel Plate
Stolen Notes, 23-25
Storm & Morgan, 131-132
Story, Francis V., 110
Stump-tail currency, 56, 65, 73, 74, 75
Subscription rates; see Bank note reporters
Sucker, 70
Suffolk Bank, Boston, 17
Swan, Samuel, 124
Swan's Bank Note List and Detector (Montgomery, Ala.), 124
Sylvester & Co., E. J., 111
Sylvester, Sylvester J., 109, 111, 125, 141
Sylvester's Bank Note and Exchange Manual, 141
Sylvester's New Reporter (New York), 111

Index

Sylvester's New Reporter, Counterfeit Detector, Bank Note Table and New York Prices Current, 111
Sylvester's Reporter and Counterfeit Detector, 110
Sylvester's Reporter, Counterfeit Detector and New York Price Current, 110
Sylvester's Reporter, Counterfeit Detector, New York Price Current and General Advertiser, 110

Taylor, H. S., 96
Taylor, S., 96
Taylor & Co., S., 96
Taylor's Gold and Silver Coin Examiner, 153
Taylor's Signature Examiner, 151
Taylor's United States Money Reporter and Gold and Silver Coin Examiner (New York), 96, 151
Tenth Ward Bank, New York, 21
Thirty shilling bills, 11
Thomas' Counterfeit Note Detector (St. Louis), 138
Thomas' reporter, 138
Thompson, Frederick F., 90, 92
Thompson, John, 49, 78, 92, 93, 95, 117, 142, 150; a dealer in lottery tickets, 78; a dealer in uncurrent bank notes, 80; agent for Yates and McIntyre, 78; as a publisher, 83; born near Peru, Mass., 78; death of, 93; description of his office, 79; failure of, 88; his locations on Wall Street, 83; his maxim, 87; his messengers, 81; his reminiscences, 80; in business in Poughkeepsie, N. Y., 78; libel action against, 90; moved from Poughkeepsie to New York City, 79; president of The Chase National Bank, 93; suit against Moses Y. Beach, 87; suit against the Union Bank, 81; suspension of, announced, 88; under criticism, 88; urged establishment of a national currency system, 90
Thompson, Samuel C., 90, 92, 93
Thompson Brothers, involved in law suit, 92
Thompson's Bank Note and Commercial Reporter (New York), 89-90, 91, 152; became a bank directory, 90; title changed, 86; the standard authority, 52, 93

Thompson's Bank Note Descriptive List, 142, 143, 144
Thompson's Bank Note Reporter, 49, 107; announcement of its first publication, 83; first subscription rates, 84
Thompson's Coin Chart Manual, 152
"Thompsonian Banks," 88
Thompsons as national bankers, The, 92
Three pound bills, 11
Tickets, as currency, 66
Tinkham, Edward I., 119
Tinkham & Co., E. I., 119
Tom's River, New Jersey, 76
Traders' Bank, Chicago, 119
Transfer press, description of present-day, 31; description of Perkins', 30
Turner, Charles, 97
Turner & Co., C., 97
Twelve shilling bills, 11

U. S. Reporter and Counterfeit Detector (Philadelphia), 129
Uncurrent bills, discount rates on, 45
Uniformity in paper currency, 39, 40
Union Bank, Ocean County, N. J., 76; Tom's River, N. J., 77
Union Bank of Kinderhook (New York), 20
Union Bank of Portsmouth, New Hampshire, 27
Union Bank of the City of New York, 80; suit by Thompson against the, 81
Union Bank Reporter Publishing Company (Cincinnati), 123, 143
"Union Banks," 20
Union Counterfeit Detector (Cincinnati), 123
United States Bank; see Bank of the United States

Van Court, John, 132, 134
Van Court's Bank Note Reporter (Philadelphia), 55
Van Court's Counterfeit Detector and Bank Note List, 132, 134, 135
Van Court's weekly sheet, 134
Virginia, notes, 44, 75; "Rags" of, 73

Waite, G. and R. (Baltimore), 7
Wall Street Banks, 80; issue of two, 76
Washington, George, 79
Waubeek Bank Plates, 19, 21

Index

Weekly Herald (New York), 47, 48
Western Counterfeit Detector, Bank Note Table, and Cincinnati Wholesale Prices Current, 120
Western Counterfeit Detector and Bank Note Table (Cincinnati), 120
Western Price Current and Weekly Bank Note Review (Pittsburgh), 137
Weybosset Bank, Providence, Rhode Island, 37
White, Francis, 2
White's Reporter and Counterfeit Detector (Cincinnati), 123, 143
Wildcat Banks and Wildcat Bank Notes, 59-77
Wildcat bounty certificates, legal tender for taxes, 62
Wildcat, definition of, 59
Willard, Edward K., 119
Willing, Thomas, president, Bank of the United States, 12
Willis & Co's Bank Note List and Counterfeit Detecter (Boston), 112-113
Wisconsin, notes, 75; stump-tail notes of, 73
Wolf bounty certificates, 62
Wolves, panthers, and wildcats, 61, 66
Work, McCouch & Co., 54, 128
Wright & Co., Geo. S., 115
Wright, Fisher & Co., 121

Yates and McIntyre, 94
Young, Caryl, 119

Zanesville Counterfeit Detector and Bank Note Reporter, 121, 140

PLATES

BANK NOTE REPORTERS   PLATE I

COUNTERFEIT NOTE — THE PATERSON BANK

BANK NOTE REPORTERS PLATE II

COUNTERFEIT NOTE —
NEWARK BANKING AND INSURANCE COMPANY

BANK NOTE REPORTERS PLATE III

SPURIOUS NOTE — THE BANK OF NEW YORK

BANK NOTE REPORTERS   PLATE IV

SPURIOUS NOTE — THE BANK OF NEW YORK

BANK NOTE REPORTERS   PLATE V

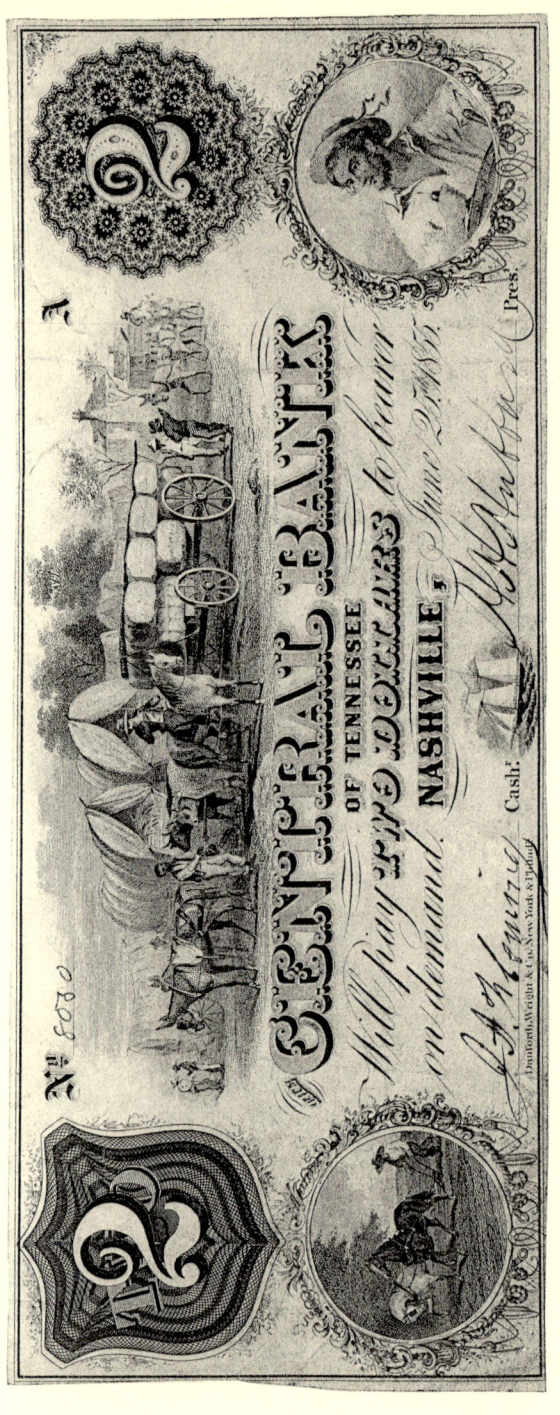

GENUINE NOTE — THE CENTRAL BANK OF TENNESSEE

BANK NOTE REPORTERS   PLATE VI

ALTERED NOTE — THE CENTRAL BANK OF TENNESSEE

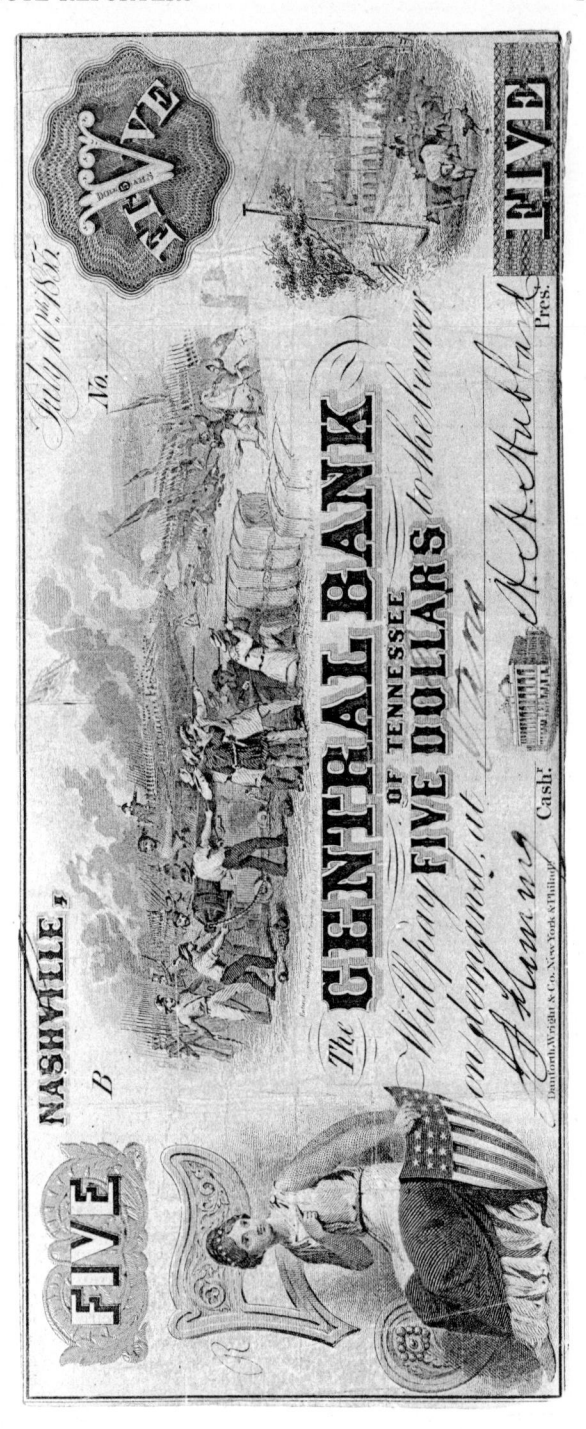

BANK NOTE REPORTERS　　　　　　　　　　　　　　PLATE VII

GENUINE NOTE — THE CENTRAL BANK OF TENNESSEE

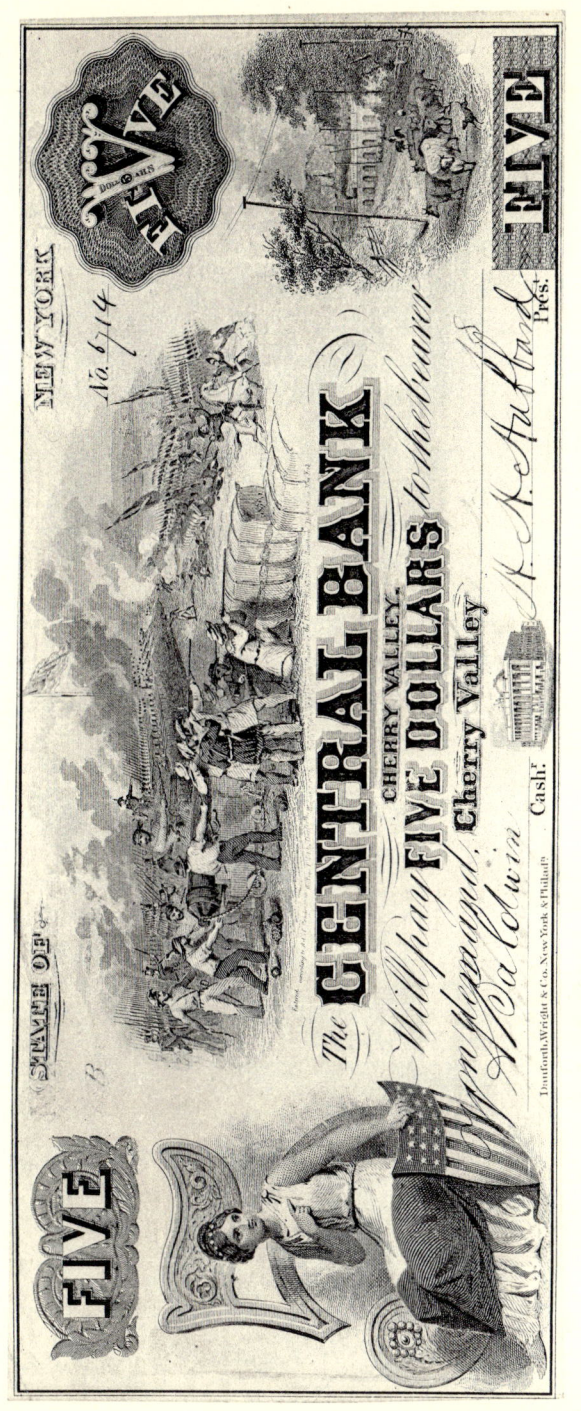

BANK NOTE REPORTERS   PLATE VIII

ALTERED NOTE — THE CENTRAL BANK OF TENNESSEE

BANK NOTE REPORTERS	PLATE IX

GENUINE NOTE —
THE NATIONAL BANK, PATERSON, NEW JERSEY

BANK NOTE REPORTERS   PLATE X

RAISED NOTE —
THE NATIONAL BANK, PATERSON, NEW JERSEY

BANK NOTE REPORTERS   PLATE XI

GENUINE NOTE — THE GLOUCESTER BANK (Obverse)

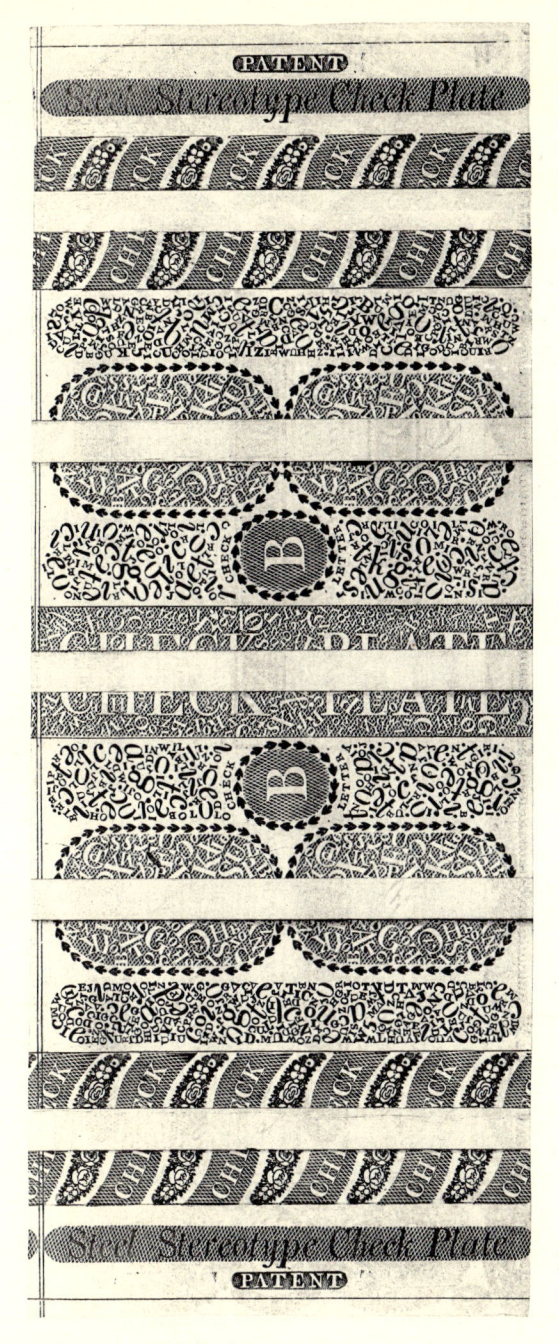

BANK NOTE REPORTERS PLATE XII

GENUINE NOTE — THE GLOUCESTER BANK (Reverse)

BANK NOTE REPORTERS PLATE XIII

POST NOTE — THE NORTH RIVER BANKING CO.

BANK NOTE REPORTERS   PLATE XIV

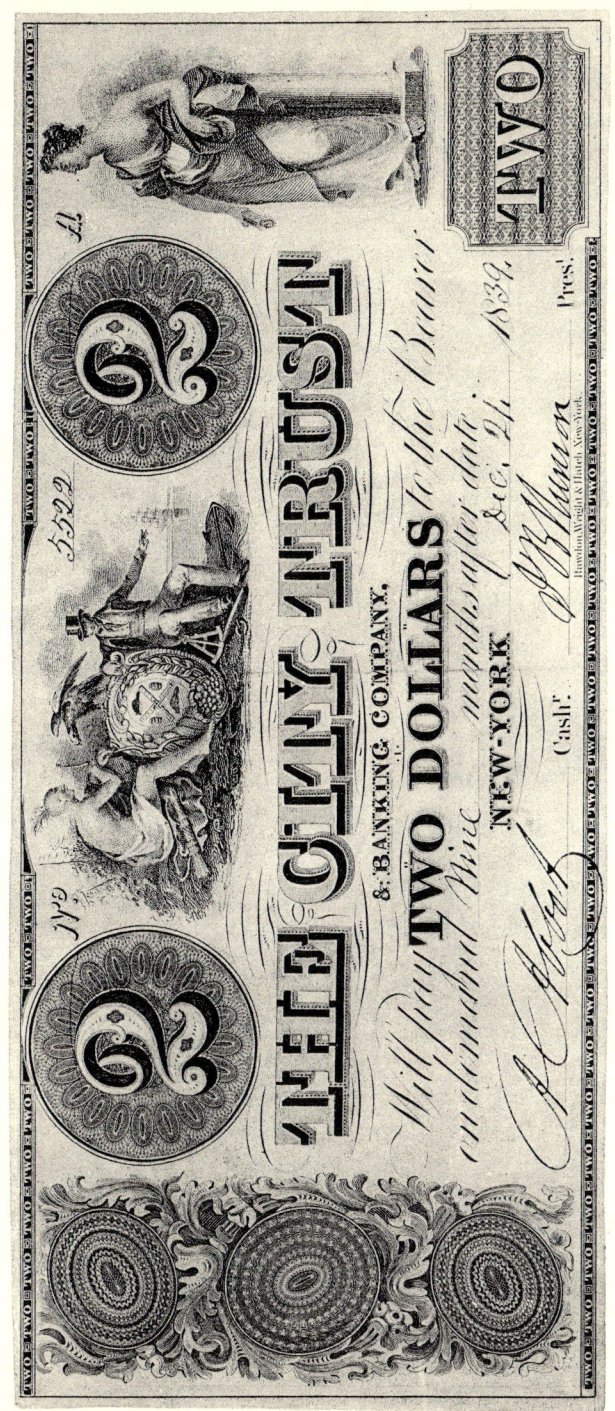

POST NOTE — THE CITY TRUST & BANKING COMPANY

BANK NOTE REPORTERS　　　　　　　　　　　　　　　　PLATE XV

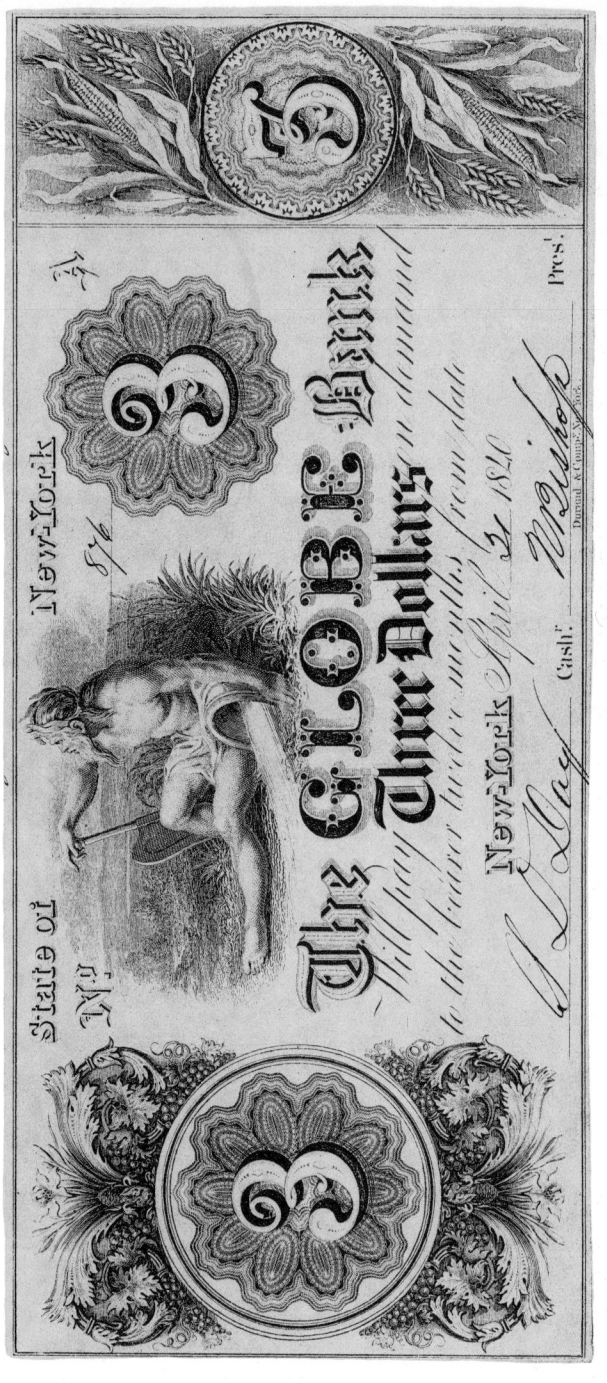

POST NOTE — THE GLOBE BANK, NEW YORK

BANK NOTE REPORTERS   PLATE XVI

POST NOTE — THE NEW-YORK LOAN COMPANY

BANK NOTE REPORTERS   PLATE XVII

NEW YORK STATE.

Merchants' & Mechanics' Bank.—Syracuse.

E. T. Lathrop, Cashier.   I. Smith, President.

Merchants' & Mechanics' Bank of Troy.

T. Taylor, Cashier.   D. T. Vail, President.

Middletown Bank.

W. M. Graham, Cashier.   Joseph Davis, President.

Mohawk Bank.

N. Switz, Cashier.   D. L. Campbell, President.

Mohawk Valley Bank.

F. E. Spinner, Cashier.   B. Carver, President.

Montgomery County Bank.

Ed. Wells, Cashier.   T. A. Stoutenburgh, Vice-President.

New York State Bank.

J. B. Plumb, Cashier.   R. H. King, Pres.

New York Security Bank.

L. D. Taylor, Cashier.   A. Hunt, President.

N. Y. Traders' Bank.

J. M. Pinckney, President.

Northern Canal Bank.

W. L. Shardlow, Jr., Cashier.   C. Rahn, President.

THE AUTOGRAPHICAL COUNTERFEIT DETECTOR
FIFTH EDITION — 1853

DYE'S BANK NOTE PLATE DELINEATOR
1855

PUBLICATIONS
THE AMERICAN NUMISMATIC SOCIETY
Broadway at 156th Street, New York 32, N. Y.

THE AMERICAN JOURNAL OF NUMISMATICS
1866–1924
Vols. 1–3: Monthly, May, 1866–April, 1870.
Vols. 4–46: Quarterly, July, 1870–October, 1912.
Vols. 47–53: Annually, 1913–1924.

With many plates, illustrations, maps and tables. The numbers necessary to complete broken sets may, in many cases, be obtained. An index to the first fifty volumes has been issued as part of Volume LI. It may be purchased separately for $3.00.

NUMISMATIC NOTES AND MONOGRAPHS

The Numismatic Notes and Monographs is a series devoted to essays and treatises on subjects relating to coins, paper money, medals and decorations. Nos. 1–109 inclusive are approximately 4½ x 6⅝ inches in size. Beginning with No. 110 the size is 6⅛ x 9 inches.

1. Sydney P. Noe. *Coin Hoards.* 1921. 47 pp. 6 pls. 50¢.
2. Edward T. Newell. *Octobols of Histiaea.* 1921. 25 pp. 2 pls. Out of print.
3. Edward T. Newell. *Alexander Hoards—Introduction and Kyparissia Hoard.* 1921. 21 pp. 2 pls. Out of print.
4. Howland Wood. *The Mexican Revolutionary Coinage, 1913–1916.* 1921. 44 pp. 26 pls. Out of print.
5. Leonidas Westervelt. *The Jenny Lind Medals and Tokens.* 1921. 25 pp. 9 pls. Out of print.
6. Agnes Baldwin. *Five Roman Gold Medallions.* 1921. 103 pp. 8 pls. $1.50.
7. Sydney P. Noe. *Medallic Work of A. A. Weinman.* 1921. 31 pp. 17 pls. Out of print.
8. Gilbert S. Perez. *The Mint of the Philippine Islands.* 1921. 8 pp. 4 pls. Out of print.
9. David Eugene Smith. *Computing Jetons.* 1921. 70 pp. 25 pls. $1.50.
10. Edward T. Newell. *The First Seleucid Coinage of Tyre.* 1921. 40 pp. 8 pls. Out of print.
11. Harrold E. Gillingham. *French Orders and Decorations.* 1922. 110 pp. 35 pls. Out of print.
12. Howland Wood. *Gold Dollars of 1858.* 1922. 7 pp. 2 pls. Out of print.
13. R. B. Whitehead. *Pre-Mohammedan Coinage of N. W. India.* 1922. 56 pp. 15 pls. Out of print.
14. George F. Hill. *Attambelos I of Characene.* 1922. 12 pp. 3 pls. Out of print.
15. M. P. Vlasto. *Taras Oikistes (A Contribution to Tarentine Numismatics).* 1922. 234 pp. 13 pls. $3.50.
16. Howland Wood. *Commemorative Coinage of the United States.* 1922. 63 pp. 7 pls. Out of print.
17. Agnes Baldwin. *Six Roman Bronze Medallions.* 1923. 39 pp. 6 pls. $1.50.
18. Howland Wood. *Tegucigalpa Coinage of 1823.* 1923. 16 pp. 2 pls. 50¢.
19. Edward T. Newell. *Alexander Hoards—II. Demanhur Hoard.* 1923. 162 pp. 8 pls. $2.50.
20. Harrold E. Gillingham. *Italian Orders of Chivalry and Medals of Honor.* 1923. 146 pp. 34 pls. Out of print.

21. Edward T. Newell. *Alexander Hoards—III. Andritsaena.* 1924. 39 pp. 6 pls. $1.00.
22. C. T. Seltman. *A Hoard from Side.* 1924. 20 pp. 3 pls. Out of print.
23. R. B. Seager. *A Cretan Coin Hoard.* 1924. 55 pp. 12 pls. $2.00.
24. Samuel R. Milbank. *The Coinage of Aegina.* 1925. 66 pp. 5 pls. $2.00.
25. Sydney P. Noe. *A Bibliography of Greek Coin Hoards.* 1925. 275 pp. $2.50.
26. Edward T. Newell. *Mithradates of Parthia and Hyspaosines of Characene.* 1925. 18 pp. 2 pls. 50¢.
27. Sydney P. Noe. *The Mende (Kaliandra) Hoard.* 1926. 73 pp. 10 pls. $2.00.
28. Agnes Baldwin. *Four Medallions from the Arras Hoard.* 1926. 36 pp. 4 pls. $1.50.
29. H. Alexander Parsons. *The Earliest Coins of Norway.* 1926. 41 pp. 1 pl. 50¢.
30. Edward T. Newell. *Some Unpublished Coins of Eastern Dynasts.* 1926. 21 pp. 2 pls. 50¢.
31. Harrold E. Gillingham. *Spanish Orders of Chivalry and Decorations of Honor.* 1926. 165 pp. 40 pls. $3.00.
32. Sydney P. Noe. *The Coinage of Metapontum.* (Part I.) 1927. 134 pp. 23 pls. $3.00.
33. Edward T. Newell. *Two Recent Egyptian Hoards—Delta and Keneh.* 1927. 34 pp. 3 pls. $1.00.
34. Edward Rogers. *The Second and Third Seleucid Coinage of Tyre.* 1927. 33 pp. 4 pls. $1.50.
35. Alfred R. Bellinger. *The Anonymous Byzantine Bronze Coinage.* 1928. 27 pp. 4 pls. $1.50.
36. Harrold E. Gillingham. *Notes on the Decorations and Medals of the French Colonies and Protectorates.* 1928. 62 pp. 31 pls. $2.00.
37. Oscar Ravel. *The "Colts" of Ambracia.* 1928. 180 pp. 19 pls. $3.00.
38. Howland Wood. *The Coinage of the Mexican Revolutionists.* 1928. 53 pp. 15 pls. $2.50.
39. Edward T. Newell. *Alexander Hoards—IV. Olympia.* 1929. 31 pp. 9 pls. $1.50.
40. Allen B. West. *Fifth and Fourth Century Gold Coins from the Thracian Coast.* 1929. 183 pp. 16 pls. $3.00.
41. Gilbert S. Perez. *The Leper Colony Currency of Culion.* 1929. 10 pp. 3 pls. 50¢.
42. Alfred R. Bellinger. *Two Hoards of Attic Bronze Coins.* 1930. 14 pp. 4 pls. 50¢.
43. D. H. Cox. *The Caparelli Hoard.* 1930. 14 pp. 2 pls. 50¢.
44. Geo. F. Hill. *On the Coins of Narbonensis with Iberian Inscriptions.* 1930. 39 pp. 6 pls. $1.00.
45. Bauman L. Belden. *A Mint in New York.* 1930. 40 pp. 4 pls. 50¢.
46. Edward T. Newell. *The Küchük Köhne Hoard.* 1931. 33 pp. 4 pls. $1.00.
47. Sydney P. Noe. *The Coinage of Metapontum. Part II.* 1931. 134 pp. 43 pls. $3.00.
48. D. W. Valentine. *The United States Half Dimes.* 1931. 79 pp. 47 pls. $5.00.
49. Alfred R. Bellinger. *Two Roman Hoards from Dura-Europos.* 1931. 66 pp. 17 pls. $1.50.
50. Geo. F. Hill. *Notes on the Ancient Coinage of Hispania Citerior.* 1931. 196 pp. 36 double pls. $4.00.
51. Alan W. Hazelton. *The Russian Imperial Orders.* 1932. 102 pp. 20 pls. $3.00.
52. O. Ravel. *Corinthian Hoards (Corinth and Arta).* 1932. 27 pp. 4 pls. $1.00.
53. Jean B. Cammann. *The Symbols on Staters of Corinthian Type (A Catalogue).* 1932. 130 pp. 14 double pls. $3.00.
54. Shirley H. Weber. *An Egyptian Hoard of the Second Century A. D.* 1932. 41 pp. 5 pls. $1.50.
55. Alfred R. Bellinger. *The Third and Fourth Dura Hoards.* 1932. 85 pp. 20 pls. $1.50.
56. Harrold E. Gillingham. *South American Decorations and War Medals.* 1932. 178 pp. 35 pls. $3.00.
57. Wm. Campbell. *Greek and Roman Plated Coins.* 1933. 226 pp. 190+pls. $3.50.
58. E. T. Newell. *The Fifth Dura Hoard.* 1933. 14 pp. 2 pls. $1.00.
59. D. H. Cox. *The Tripolis Hoard.* 1933. 61 pp. 8 pls. 2 maps. $1.50.

60. E. T. Newell. *Two Hoards from Minturno*. 1933. 38 pp. 5 pls. $1.00.
61. Howland Wood. *The Gampola Larin Hoard*. 1934. 84 pp. 10 double pls. $3.00.
62. J. G. Milne. *The Melos Hoard of 1907*. 1934. 19 pp. 1 pl. $1.00.
63. A. F. Pradeau. *The Mexican Mints of Alamos and Hermosillo*. 1934. 73 pp. illus. 3 pls. $1.50.
64. E. T. Newell. *A Hoard from Siphnos*. 1934. 17 pp. 1 pl. 50¢.
65. C. H. V. Sutherland. *Romano-British Imitations of Bronze Coins of Claudius I*. 1935. 35 pp. 8 double pls. $2.00.
66. Harrold E. Gillingham. *Ephemeral Decorations*. 1935. 40 pp. 11 pls. $2.00.
67. Sawyer McA. Mosser. *A Bibliography of Byzantine Coin Hoards*. 1935. 116 pp. $1.50.
68. Edward T. Newell. *Five Greek Bronze Coin Hoards*. 1935. 67 pp. 9 double pls. $2.00.
69. Alfred R. Bellinger. *The Sixth, Seventh and Tenth Dura Hoards*. 1935. 75 pp. 5 pls. $1.00.
70. Frederick O. Waage. *Greek Bronze Coins from a Well at Megara*. 1935. 42 pp. 3 pls. $1.00.
71. Sydney P. Noe. *The Thurian Di-Staters*. 1935. 68 pp. 11 double pls. $2.00.
72. John Walker. *The Coinage of the Second Saffarid Dynasty in Sistan*. 1936. 46 pp. 4 double pls. $1.00.
73. Edward T. Newell. *The Seleucid Coinage of Tyre*. 1936. 34 pp. 5 pls. $1.00.
74. Margaret Crosby and Emily Grace. *An Achaean League Hoard*. 1936. 44 pp. 4 pls. $1.50.
75. Agnes Baldwin Brett. *Victory Issues of Syracuse after 413 B.C.* 1936. 6 pp. 2 pls. 50¢.
76. Edward T. Newell. *The Pergamene Mint under Philetaerus*. 1936. 34 pp. 10 pls. $2.50.
77. Charles C. Torrey. *Aramaic Graffiti on Coins of Demanhur*. 1937. 13 pp. 2 pls. $1.00.
78. Sydney P. Noe. *A Bibliography of Greek Coin Hoards. (Second Edition)*. 1937. 362 pp. $4.00.
79. Naphtali Lewis. *A Hoard of Folles from Seltz (Alsace)*. 1937. 81 pp. 5 pls. $2.00.
80. Harold Mattingly and W. P. D. Stebbing. *The Richborough Hoard of 'Radiates.' 1931*. 1938. 118 pp. 15 pls. $2.50.
81. Alfred R. Bellinger. *Coins from Jerash. 1928–1934*. 1938. 141 pp. 9 pls. $2.50.
82. Edward T. Newell. *Miscellanea Numismatica: Cyrene to India*. 1938. 101 pp. 6 pls. $2.00.
83. David M. Bullowa. *The Commemorative Coinage of the United States 1892–1938*. 1938. 192 pp. 10 pls. $2.50.
84. Edward T. Newell. *Late Seleucid Mints in Ake-Ptolemais and Damascus*. 1939. 107 pp. 17 pls. $2.00.
85. Alfred R. Bellinger. *The Eighth and Ninth Dura Hoards*. 1939. 92 pp. 13 pls. $2.00.
86. Harrold E. Gillingham. *Counterfeiting in Colonial Pennsylvania*. 1939. 52 pp. 2 pls. $1.00.
87. George C. Miles. *A Byzantine Weight Validated by al-Walid*. 1939. 11 pp. 1 pl. 50¢.
88. Jaime Gonzalez. *A Puerto Rican Counterstamp*. 1940. 21 pp. 2 pls. $1.00.
89. Harrold E. Gillingham. *Mexican Decorations of Honour*. 1940. 53 pp. 17 pls. $2.00.
90. Donald F. Brown. *Temples of Rome as Coin Types*. 1940. 51 pp. 9 pls. $1.50.
91. Eunice Work. *The Early Staters of Heraclea Lucaniae*. 1940. 40 pp. 8 pls. $2.00.
92. D. H. Cox. *A Tarsus Coin Collection in the Adana Museum*. 1941. 67 pp. 12 pls. $2.00.
93. Herbert E. Ives. *Foreign Imitations of the English Noble*. 1941. 36 pp. 5 pls. $1.50.
94. Louis C. West. *Gold and Silver Coin Standards in the Roman Empire*. 1941. 199 pp. $1.50.
95. Arthur D. McIlvaine. *The Silver Dollars of the United States of America*. 1941. 36 pp. 1 folded pl. $1.00.

96. J. G. Milne. *Kolophon and its Coinage. A Study.* 1941. 113 pp. 19 double pls. $2.50.
97. Sawyer McA. Mosser. *The Endicott Gift of Greek and Roman Coins.* 1941. 65 pp. 9 pls. $1.50.
98. Edgar Erskine Hume. *The Medals of the United States Army Medical Department and Medals Honoring Army Medical Officers.* 1942. 146 pp. 23 pls. $3.00.
99. Phares O. Sigler. *Sycee Silver.* 1943. 37 pp. 6 pls. $1.00.
100. Sydney P. Noe. *The Castine Deposit: An American Hoard.* 1942. 37 pp. 4 pls. $1.00.
101. H. F. Bowker. *A Numismatic Bibliography of the Far East.* 1943. 144 pp. $1.50.
102. Sydney P. Noe. *The New England and Willow Tree Coinages of Massachusetts.* 1943. 56 pp. 16 pls. $3.00.
103. Nai Chi Chang. *An Inscribed Chinese Ingot of the XII Century A. D.* 1944. 9 pp. 2 pls. 50¢.
104. George L. McKay. *Early American Currency.* 1944. 85 pp. 27 pls. Out of print.
105. Edward T. Newell. *The Byzantine Hoard of Lagbe.* 1945. 22 pp. 8 pls. $1.00.
106. James C. Risk. *British Orders and Decorations.* 1945. 124 pp. 76 pls. $4.00.
107. Bluma L. Trell. *The Temple of Artemis at Ephesos.* 1945. 71 pp. 28 pls. $2.00.
108. Karel O. Castelin. *The Coinage of Rhesaena in Mesopotamia.* 1946. 11 pp. 17 pls. $2.00.
109. Aline A. Boyce. *Coins of Tingi with Latin Legends.* 1947. 27 pp. 5 pls. $1.00.
110. Sydney P. Noe. *The Oak Tree Coinage of Massachusetts.* 1947. 23 pp. 10 pls. $1.50.
111. George C. Miles. *Early Arabic Glass Weights and Stamps.* 1948. 168 pp. 14 pls. $5.00.
112. Philip V. Hill. *"Barbarous Radiates:" Imitations of Third-Century Roman Coins.* 1949. 44 pp. 4 pls. $2.00.
113. Richard N. Frye. *Notes on the Early Coinage of Transoxiana.* 1949. 49 pp. 1 pl. $2.00.

MUSEUM NOTES

The American Numismatic Society Museum Notes is a publication consisting principally of brief notes and papers on items in the Society's collections.

    I—1946.   106 pp.   23 pls. $1.50.
   II—1947.   118 pp.   19 pls. $1.50.
  III—1948.   154 pp.   26 pls. $5.00.

NUMISMATIC STUDIES

This series accommodates works of full book length, 7¾ x 10¾ inches in size.

1. Edward T. Newell. *The Coinage of the Eastern Seleucid Mints from Seleucus I to Antiochus III.* 1938. 307 pp. 56 pls. $6.00.
2. George C. Miles. *The Numismatic History of Rayy.* 240 pp. 6 pls. $4.00.
3. Alfred R. Bellinger. *The Syrian Tetradrachms of Caracalla and Macrinus.* 1940. 116 pp. 26 pls. $5.00.
4. Edward T. Newell. *The Coinage of the Western Seleucid Mints from Seleucus I to Antiochus III.* 1941. 450 pp. 86 pls. $10.00.
5. Jocelyn M. C. Toynbee. *Roman Medallions.* 1944. 268 pp. 49 pls. Out of print.

NUMISMATIC LITERATURE

A quarterly listing of current numismatic publications with abstracts of their content. Subscription price to non-members is $2.00 per year postpaid. Single current issues, $.50 each.

George H. Clapp and Howard R. Newcomb. *The United States Cents of the Years 1795, 1796, 1797 and 1800.* 1947. 74 pp. 4 photographic pls. Bound in cloth. $10.00.
Edward T. Newell. *The Coinages of Demetrius Poliorcetes.* London. Oxford University Press. 1927. 174 pp. 18 pls. $5.00.